Battlefield Doc

Battlefield Doc
Memoirs of a Korean War Combat Medic

WILLIAM J. "DOC" ANDERSON

MOONBRIDGE PUBLICATIONS
St. Louis, Missouri
2015

Battlefield Doc: Memoirs of a Korean War Combat Medic

All rights reserved.
Copyright ©2015 by William J. Anderson

Cover design and interior by Cathy Wood
Historic cover photo courtesy Library of Congress, Prints and Photographs Division
Drawing of "Doc" Anderson by Glenn Cheung ©2015

Other photos and memorabilia from William J. "Doc" Anderson unless noted.

Printed in the United States of America
No part of this book may be reproduced or transmitted in any form without written permission of the publisher, except for brief passages in connection with a review.

An early version of "Baptism by Fire" was published in the anthology *Proud to Be: Writing by American Warriors, Volume 2*, edited by Susan Swartwout, published by Southeast Missouri State Press, 2013, with Missouri Humanities Council and Warriors Arts Alliance.

ISBN: 978-0-9772323-3-8
Library of Congress Control Number: 2015950202

Moonbridge Publications LLC
701 Simmons Ave
St. Louis, MO 63122

Publisher's Note: The purpose of this book is to provide information and firsthand knowledge on the subject matter covered as best remembered by the author and through research to verify and enhance the historical perspective of the author's personal experience. This is not a historical document.

Dedication

This book is dedicated to the many medics and corpsmen who gave their all 24/7 in our wars and military conflicts

AND

A special acknowledgment for those who served during the Korean War
June 25, 1950 – July 27, 1953

ACCLAIM FOR "BATTLEFIELD DOC"

As you read, you see him put on his aid kits. Listen to the cries for "Doc." This is a must read for those who have never experienced the horrors of combat. It is a story about all combat medics. It tells of their endurance and heroism. – *Earl Link, retired Marine*

These stories are snapshots through the eyes of one heroic and courageous combat medic. His close friends convinced him that the life of a combat medic should be told. He is finally sharing what he saw firsthand and what has haunted him for all these years. – *Robin Dahle*

William J. Anderson, the "Battlefield Doc," provides us with a glimpse into the life of a young medic during the Korean Conflict. He is one of the unsung heroes we tend to hear little about. His recollections serve not only as a valuable part of military history, but as a reminder of the humanity and inhumanity of war. – *Deborah L. Marshall, founder of the Missouri Warrior Writers Project/Warriors Arts Alliance.*

This book is an accurate and personal description of combat as experienced by a combat medic. Few people know much about the work of combat medics and the fearful and threatening situations they are exposed to in war. Providing urgent care under incoming artillery fire or infantry assaults or while running patrols into no-man's land are extraordinary accomplishments. Medics are often more exposed to danger than other soldiers engaging in the action.

Having served as an infantryman in Korea, I can attest to the high trust we had for our medics—they were always there for us regardless of the danger or difficult circumstances. As described in this memoir, the reader will understand the important role that medics play. The extreme value of combat medics will be attested to by every combat infantryman. – *James N. Butcher, author of Korea: Traces of a forgotten war, 2013, Hellgate Press*

TABLE OF CONTENTS

CHAPTER 1 I WAS A COMBAT MEDIC 3

CHAPTER 2 BAPTISM BY FIRE 10

CHAPTER 3 FIVE DAYS OF HELL 17

CHAPTER 4 SHADOWS OF DEATH 23

CHAPTER 5 TILL HELL FREEZES OVER 29

CHAPTER 6 PITCHFORKS AND BROOMSTICKS 34

CHAPTER 7 JITTERY AND JUMPY 39

CHAPTER 8 DEATH, DEATH, EVERYWHERE DEATH 46

CHAPTER 9 BOOT PRINTS IN THE SNOW 52

CHAPTER 10 EENY, MEENY, MINY, MOE 57

CHAPTER 11 BADASS BOYS 63

CHAPTER 12 DAWN OF ANOTHER DAY 71

CHAPTER 13 CODE NAME L-7 78

CHAPTER 14 QUIET FOR A MOMENT 85

CHAPTER 15 SLIPPING AND SLIDING 90

CHAPTER 16 MONSOON RAINS 94

CHAPTER 17 THE STENCH OF BLOOD AND DEATH 97

CHAPTER 18 EAGLE'S NEST 103

CHAPTER 19 PRISONERS NO MORE 110

CHAPTER 20 SEE YOU IN HEAVEN 115

CHAPTER 21	HORRIBLE BLOODBATH	120
CHAPTER 22	LUCK OR FATE	126
CHAPTER 23	BAYONETS AND KNIVES	136
CHAPTER 24	GREENHORNS NO MORE	139
CHAPTER 25	HAUNTING EYES	143
CHAPTER 26	OUTPOST NO MORE	149
CHAPTER 27	NAPALM BURNING	155
CHAPTER 28	EAGLE ONE	159
CHAPTER 29	BEHIND ENEMY LINES	167
CHAPTER 30	BY WAY OF THE KNIFE	175
CHAPTER 31	DEATH SURROUNDS ME	181
CHAPTER 32	AN ENEMY IN ITSELF	187
CHAPTER 33	AGAINST ALL ODDS	195
CHAPTER 34	CODE RED	201
CHAPTER 35	UNBELIEVABLE CARNAGE	206
CHAPTER 36	LAST WORDS	213
	BATTLEFIELD PRAYER	216
	GLOSSARY	221

PREFACE

William J. Anderson, Korean War combat medic of Medical Company C, 14th Infantry Regiment, 25th Infantry Division, was known as "Doc" during the war, along with all the other "docs" who were Army medics or Navy corpsmen. He served from fall 1951 to spring 1953. He is now also known as "Coach," as he became a pro tennis player and coach in his life after the war years. This book was created mostly from notes Doc kept while in Korea and from additional stories he told me. I researched Korean War history to verify information and add details for better understanding, but this book is meant as a testimony to the lives of combat medics and front line soldiers and is not a historical document. Troopers going home from their tour of duty carried pages of Doc's notes with them, and once stateside, mailed them to his family home.

Doc never imagined his notes would become a book, so he did not include dates or place names in his writings. The stories are ordered by season and by best guess as to time frame. As a medic, Doc always carried a watch and a thermometer, so his notes contain references to time and temperature. He wanted to use military time to give a better feel for life on the battlefield, so occasionally I included the 12-hour time in parenthesis for readers not used to 24-hour time.

Although Doc rewrote his notes by hand after he recovered physically from the war, he kept them as a matter of personal and historical interest. Years later, his friends read some of his notes and insisted he turn his experiences into a book. I hope readers will feel they are right beside Doc in the trenches. This is what "The Forgotten War" was like for the fighting soldiers on the ground and for the combat medics and corpsmen trying to save them. These men are heroic, although likely none will admit to it. Mostly, I agree with Doc that "people need to know that life is hell when you are in a war zone."

– Linda Austin, editor and publisher

ACKNOWLEDGMENTS

I am infinitely grateful to Robin Dahle for his friendship, support, and advice.

Many thanks to:
Robin Link who encouraged me to write this book

Earl Link, a former Marine and friend whose keen eye spotted things I had missed

Mark Brookshier, a former Navy corpsman, for all his help with this project

Polly Bradshaw for helping with the difficult job of typing up my handwritten notes

Linda Austin for editing and publishing

And I give thanks to those who served, for without whom I would have neither begun nor finished this book.

FROM THE AUTHOR

Not much has been written about a time and place I call "Hell on Earth." I'm writing about the Korean War so young people will know about the pain and suffering and of the casualties of war, especially of the front line soldiers. My generation was part of that hell on earth that was fought from 1950 to 1953. I will do my part not to let it become "The Forgotten War."

Most stories of war are told about the killing, but few are about saving lives. I was told some years back by a veteran of both World War II and the Korean War that he thought combat medics never got enough credit for what they did in those wars. They thought first of saving lives on the battlefield, without thinking twice about their own. In his mind they were all true heroes. I thanked this veteran for his kind words and told him I didn't think of considering myself a hero. I had a job to do, and I did it to the best of my ability.

Often it was hard to go back in time after all the years spent trying to forget what happened. These are my experiences as I remember them. I rewrote my notes the best I could—some had faded from rain or snow. There may be minor inaccuracies. On the front line I kept busy aiding the wounded and taking care of other job duties. I wrote when I could find a minute. I didn't think to write down dates and did not usually know the names of places, but the 25th Infantry troops I was usually attached to as a medic were at the Punchbowl, Heartbreak Ridge, Pork Chop Hill, Kumhwa Valley, Chorwon, Mungdung-Ni, Kaesong, and other areas along the 38th Parallel. I may not remember the exact locations or everyone's names, but I'll never forget those places, or the faces. They still haunt me.

Korea was truly a story of unambiguous heroism in which the seemingly impossible was routinely achieved.

—William "Doc" Anderson

To all the men and women
who have lost their lives for our country,
I say thanks.
When I see that American flag
flying high in the sky,
my heart and my thoughts
are with those who sacrificed all.
Our flag represents
those brave and heroic soldiers.

—William "Doc" Anderson

Battlefield Doc

by William J. "Doc" Anderson

Doc Anderson by Glenn Cheung

CHAPTER 1

I WAS A COMBAT MEDIC

"Doc, am I going to die?"

"Hang in there, it's a piece of cake." I wrapped a tourniquet high on the soldier's thigh to stop the bleeding. Carefully holding the end of a large, jagged piece of shrapnel, I slowly eased it out of the trooper's thigh. He winced, but gave me a thumbs-up. "You're okay, Doc!" I cleaned the wound, dabbed on some ointment, then bandaged it up. I gave a shot of morphine for the pain and tagged the man as WIA—wounded in action. As the litter-bearers took him back to our makeshift aid station, I went on to the next cry of "Doc!"

There are moments you will always remember, like your first kiss, your first car, your first job. This day stands in my memory… the first time I heard the desperate calls for "Medic!" or "Doc!" The first time I patched up a wounded battlefield soldier. Will he live, or will he die? On my first day of combat duty, I aided some thirty-five wounded. All in a day's work.

"Overwhelming responsibilities" was what I found when the time came for me to do this job. All my training stateside at various Army medical schools would come front and center in caring for and aiding our troops, especially the training in a pitch dark gymnasium, feeling our way to aid "wounded" volunteers after our eyes adjusted to the darkness. Earning the First Aid merit badge back in Boy Scouts turned out to be paramount, too. Being a Boy Scout saved my life and helped me save others in Korea many times over. All I learned from earning three sashes full of badges and roughing it on tough bivouacs really helped.

Death and severe injury were ever-present dangers for medics. We were easy targets at times, like sitting ducks in a shooting gallery, because we were often out in the open while aiding the wounded. The enemy troops would zero in on us. But, when someone yelled "Doc," you took off running or crawling to whoever needed help. You just hoped to make it in time.

I had a few titles to go with the job: Bed Pan Commando, Pill-Pusher, Steward of the Wards, "Shanker" Mechanic, and some I dare not say. I went in as a private and somewhere along the line became a sergeant. I was with Medical Company C with the 25th Infantry Division, nicknamed Tropic Lightning, and usually attached to the 14th Infantry Regiment, the Golden Dragons. As a medic, I felt I was one part each doctor, nurse, mom, dad, sister, brother, and chaplain. Often the badly wounded clearly needed a shoulder to lean on.

I felt the sting of war in the trenches, foxholes, and bunkers on the battlefields and behind enemy lines. I removed shrapnel and bullets from the flesh of young men. I often had to ignore my own safety to treat our injured troops. We were in a hellhole place called Korea. You did what you had to do. The riskiest thing to do was to not act. I would rather try and fail than not try at all.

Sometimes I was sent to different units in the 25th Division and to different outfits, like to the Marines at the Punchbowl, but otherwise I was busy doing my work and went where I was told without asking questions. The day could be as dim as evening from all the smoke and dust from explosions and the ground could be blasted clean of trees and shrubs, and many times we were on the move in the dark. I could care less what the hills were called, they were all hell to me.

The whole of Korea is a peninsula, with mountains to the north and east and plains to the south and west. The entire country is about the size of Utah. Korea has four seasons, like my home state of Missouri. The North Korean winters were roughly from November through March. The summers were extremely hot and humid, with monsoon rains in July and August, but April and May and September and October were nice and mild. In the years during the Korean War, the summers got to be 100 degrees and hotter, with humidity in the 90 percent range, and the monsoons brought torrential rain and mud. The North Korean winters were bitter cold, with winds howling in from Siberia and Manchuria in the north. Sometimes the temperature would get to 40 to 50 degrees below zero, without factoring in the wind chill.

The "conflict" in Korea began on June 25, 1950, when North Korea attacked South Korea, although they still argue about who started it. The United States, with support from fifteen United Nations countries, joined in to keep anti-communist South Korea from being overtaken by communist North Korea. China sent in troops to help North Korea, and the Soviet Union provided supplies. This was the first military action of the Cold War, that time of tension between the U.S. and the Soviet Union.

The Korean War to this day has never legally ended. On July 27, 1953, North Korea and the UN Command signed an armistice ending the hostilities, but North Korea and South Korea have never signed a peace treaty. Both countries are still technically at war and a two-and-a-half-mile-wide demilitarized buffer zone separates them. Over three million lives were lost during the Korean War, mostly North Korean and Chinese, including over a million civilians from both Koreas. According to the U.S. Army Center of Military History, over 33,000 Americans died in combat and thousands of men are still missing. Over 103,000 Americans were wounded in action.

In the Korean War, a wounded soldier could get medical care fast. Medics and corpsmen, known to all as "docs," were on the front lines. None of us were physicians, but we had extensive first-aid training. Medics were trained at various Army medical schools, corpsmen at various Navy medical institutions. We stopped bleeding with tourniquets—we called them snakes, or worms. We administered IVs and blood plasma and gave morphine shots to dull pain and prevent shock. I kept a big rubber band around my helmet to hold the shots. Morphine on one side, tetanus on the other, penicillin in back. Sulfa powder and ointments helped keep wounds from getting infected. We carried booklets of EMTs, the emergency medical tags, to write out a soldier's name, rank, serial number, age, religion, blood type, military outfit, and brief summary of treatment given. The wounded were tagged WIA—wounded in action. The dead were tagged KIA—killed in action. Litter-bearers carried the wounded on stretchers to waiting jeeps for a ride to the battalion aid station, or BAS. Those were usually a few hundred yards behind the front line. The MASH, or Mobile Army Surgical Hospital units, for the most part were some miles back in the rear. The badly wounded were taken by helicopter to MASH for the really big jobs done by surgeons, doctors, and nurses.

Helicopters were used for medevac. The H-13 Bell helicopter, famous from the movie and TV series *M*A*S*H*, had a two-seater cockpit with a plastic bubble dome over it. The H-13 was a flying ambulance. With stretchers carrying the wounded attached to its ski-skids outside, the chopper flew to the BAS or to the MASH. It was a windy ride for all, as well as for the combat medic who many times had to hook himself up outside the chopper to maintain the IV line and keep up the medical care. The ride was dangerous and scary for all, including the pilot. Small arms fire came from everywhere, and the enemy aimed at choppers coming up to the front line. The choppers hovered while the wounded were strapped on, and then took off.

Sometimes I had to ride outside the chopper in zero-degree weather. Working on a wounded soldier in zero weather in and of itself is a challenge, to say the least. Many times my hands were numb because I could only do so much with gloves on. I always wondered how the troops ever made it in such horrible conditions. Of course, some didn't. As a combat medic, I had to deal with three enemies:

heatstroke in the summer, frostbite in the winter, and the human enemy all the time.

In the trenches, it was the medic or corpsman who made sick-call rounds, giving out aspirin for fevers or colds as well as for treating the pain from wounds. The medic would lance and patch up blisters, attend to trench foot—an infection from the foot being wet and cold too long—and frostbitten limbs, etc. He dealt with all kinds of injuries, serious or slight, day in and day out. Not all injuries were battle wounds, some were just from accidents. Medics also went on patrols, missions, raids, and ambushes behind enemy lines, often without weapons. And, by the way, they were on call twenty-four hours a day, seven days a week. No complaining about interrupted break times. Knowing each of our troops' medical make-up was another part of our job. We had to know what they could or could not take as far as pills and shots were concerned. We medics tried to go over this together about once a week, when possible.

There were times, though not many, when it was so quiet I could hear crickets. Then during my morning or evening rounds, I could hear the troops talking it up, mostly just shooting the bull. Sometimes I would hand out mail, and talk might turn to what if something would happen to them on a patrol or mission. They wanted me to write to their families and tell them how they died. This was the Red Cross's job, but I agreed to do it. Some of the troopers wanted me to tell their families personally. How does one say such things? With me being twenty-one years old, and I guess also being a medic, they thought I knew everything. After all, most of them were only boys in their teens. Some had even lied about their age to sign up to fight.

I wrote short and to the point. That, I felt, was the only way the families would want it. Plus, I had promised the troopers I'd be honest; I owed them that. I hate to tell you how many letters I wrote. That was really hard to do. I learned in medical school not to get close to any of the troops. One day a soldier is here and the next day he's gone. Death plays no favorites.

No man's land is the real estate between the front line of one side and the other. Death was a constant companion for those troopers pulling duty on the front line. They hunkered down in snake-like trenches winding for miles on end, in the bitter cold of winter or in the sweltering humidity of summer. Artillery and mortar shells landed all around. They call that incoming mail. Bullets flew in all directions. The front line troopers' eyes were on that no man's land. They knew the enemy might cross at any moment.

As a combat medic, I learned one helluva lot of life lessons: patience, discipline, and an understanding that many things happen for a reason. I found two things were a must—you must not panic, and you must have steady hands. This helps keep people alive. In later years, many World War II veterans and Korean War veterans who fought in combat would tell me, "We owe our lives to those medics and corpsmen."

I often think and pray for those I aided. I wonder which ones made it out of that hellhole, and where they are and what they're doing today. I doubt our paths will ever cross again, but I will always remember them even if I have forgotten their names. In my mind, they were all true American heroes. When I see our American flag waving high and I hear "God Bless America," "America the Beautiful," "The Star Spangled Banner," or "The Battle Hymn of the Republic," I get chills.

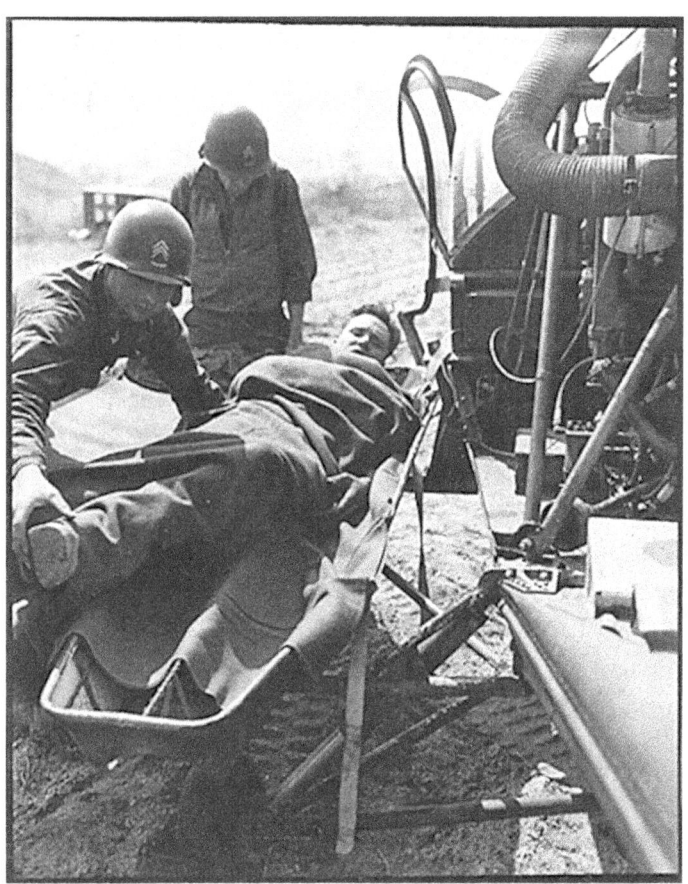
Library of Congress, Prints and Photographs Division

CHAPTER 2

BAPTISM BY FIRE

We had landed on the east coast of North Korea, "Land of the Morning Calm," about an hour ago. The moon was full and the air was warm and heavy for a September night. The commanding officer, the CO, was a captain with two silver bars. He asked if I had any aspirin for his headache. As I handed him a couple, gunfire popped in the distance and flares shot into the sky.

We were about half a mile or so from the main line of resistance, the MLR, also known as the front line. We were to relieve the company there. All my medical training was about to come into play. Was I scared? You bet your tootsies. By the light of the moon I saw what was left of jeeps, trucks, tanks, and buildings blown up all over the area. To my right was the battalion aid station where I would be heading to load up my two aid kits with supplies and medicine for our medical aid bunker.

We made it up the hill to the MLR. Under cover of artillery and mortar fire, one at a time, man by man, we relieved the other company. The medics said they had really taken a beating the last four days. They wished us luck and yelled back as they headed down the hill, "Keep your heads and asses down!"

It took us about two hours to get settled into our new home—if you can call bunkers and sandbagged trenches home. We had sleeping cots made of the heavy commo wire used for our field telephone lines. The wire was wrapped in black tape and crisscrossed to form a kind of netting. On top of that we put blankets. Our pillows were small blankets rolled up and tied together. Our underground medical aid bunker was between the command post and a group of four tanks attached to our sector of the MLR. In our company we had twelve medics including myself, and twenty-four litter-bearers roamed up and down our sector of trenches and bunkers.

By midnight everyone had dug in for the night. Everything had gone without a hitch. A flare shot up every now and then. In the valley below, a few rounds sputtered from automatic weapons. I tried to get a little shut-eye, but at 0330 hours a soldier came into our medical bunker saying he had a sore throat and maybe a fever as well. I took his temperature and sure enough he had a fever—101 degrees. I swabbed his throat and gave him two aspirins plus some throat lozenges for later. He sacked out in our bunker until morning. When he woke, I told him to see me in two days and sent him back to his post. So far, all was well on the home front.

The CO met with our medical staff of twelve, the litter-bearers, plus all squad and platoon leaders, all of us crowded into his bunker. He said, "Each of us has a duty to carry out. Do them as a team and we'll all get out of this God-forsaken land alive." He told us medics, "You keep us alive, we'll keep you alive." Looking at me, he said, "Doc, will you lead the medical staff?" I agreed, but I don't know why he picked me except that I was a little older than the others. Older meaning I was twenty-one, but I had done well in training and maybe he'd heard about that, and that I had a little experience before, too. After high school, I was the athletic director at the St. James Recreation Center in Kansas City, Missouri, and had taped up many ankles and fixed up many cuts and scrapes. I went back and forth to Camp LeJeune for training since I was in the Marine Reserves. I finished up with the Reserves, but when this Korean "conflict" broke out, I was drafted. I said, "Hey, you said I was done!"

Like us medics, many of our troops were new to combat as

well. We had three platoons to our company. The platoons each had three squads of fourteen men plus four medics, eight litter-bearers, one radioman, one interpreter, and one officer, rounding it out to fifty-seven men in each platoon. We medics spent most of the day seeing to the troops' medical needs. I passed out a few pills and gave a few penicillin shots. I bandaged a few who had some scrapes and bruises. The day had been more or less quiet. We went up and down our front line position talking with the troops. We also met with the tankers. We would take care of their medical needs as well. The tank drivers would fight with us, but they had objectives of their own to follow. We medics, along with our litter-bearers, spent time familiarizing ourselves with the surrounding terrain.

The sun had gone down when the CO sent word to my platoon leader, a lieutenant, that he had planned a recon—a reconnaissance patrol. We were going over our MLR and down the valley into no man's land—that land between the front lines of us good guys and the bad guys. The bad guys were the North Korean gooks and their Chinese Chink friends. Our platoon would go first, at zero hour—2100 hours (9:00 p.m.). He wished us luck.

This would be our first chance to test our so-called bulletproof vests. They would not stop a direct hit, but if the bullet came from far away it should only knock us down. The vests were heavy and hot, and were mostly to protect us against shrapnel. As of now, combat medics were the only ones issued them. Our litter-bearers and troops were to get theirs in another month or so. Medics would be out in the open working on the wounded, so the vests would give us needed protection.

We had two hours to kill. The Lieutenant asked me to check out our interpreter, an ROK—Republic of Korea—army trooper. He had a cut on his leg. The Lieutenant also gave me the password and counter for the night's patrol—*iron* and *fist*. I was to make sure the other medics and litter-bearers knew them. The password was our passport for getting in and out of our MLR.

After tending to our interpreter, I helped our troops tape down their dog tags. We had to make sure they wouldn't rattle and give our position away. I also helped blacken everyone's faces and hands with special ointment, so they wouldn't glow in the moonlight. Then it was zero hour, when the rubber hits the road. We gave the password to the guards, moved through a gap in the rolls of barbed wire marking our MLR, crept down through our minefield into the valley below, and entered no man's land. Making our way through the minefield was an anxious time, especially in the dark. We went single file, left hand on the left shoulder of the guy in front. Several wires, about twenty yards apart with color-coded flags attached, draped down the hill. Our safe path flag color for the day was green. We slid our right hands along that wire as we descended the hill. One misstep would be disaster. At the end of the descent, we dropped the guide wire back to the ground.

The Lieutenant had the platoon get into a diamond formation as we got closer to the other side of no man's land. That meant the Lieutenant, us four medics, our eight litter-bearers, our interpreter, and our radioman were all in the middle of the formation of troops for added protection, in case the enemy had something up their sleeves, like hiding in the brush waiting to shoot us. We passed through into the enemy's half of no man's land—so far so good. We were about one thousand yards from the enemy-held position, the moon shining in and out of thick clouds. Suddenly we heard screaming and the enemy came running toward us at full speed, rifles waving above their heads. We had been ambushed!

We hit the ground. The small group of enemy was about fifty yards away, still coming but not firing their weapons. Our point man blasted away with his big Browning Automatic Rifle. The other men lobbed hand grenades and fired away with automatic weapons. The enemy kept coming, screaming and yelling and waving their weapons. Still they did not fire. They were about twenty-five yards away and dropping like flies.

All went silent. The Lieutenant motioned to a squad leader to round up four others and check things out. They disappeared into the dark as clouds covered the moon, and returned shortly to report it was okay to move forward. Low and behold, all twenty-eight enemy lay dead. But none of them were soldiers. They were old men, farmers, and other civilians. Those weren't rifles they'd been waving, they were pitchforks and broomsticks. We had heard about things like this. We felt bad in a way. How could we know they weren't carrying guns? This was war—it was us or them.

The Lieutenant told us to be on full alert and in formation. We moved forward, but at a slower pace. We were about three hundred yards from enemy lines when the enemy came. Again out in the darkness we heard screaming and yelling, this time joined by bugles, whistles, banging drums, and pounding horses' hooves. Bullets hissed and zinged. Chinese Communist and North Korean forces rushed in from the hills in front of us. We were outnumbered!

We medics crawled to our assigned areas in the middle of the formation. I told myself this was for all the marbles. Our troops went into action. Hell broke out from both sides. The rapid burping sound of enemy submachine guns filled the valley floor. We were hit by mortar rounds. Lieutenant got the coordinates of the enemy's hill in front of us and called in for artillery fire plus two more squads for backup. Until then we were on our own.

After an hour or so in combat, I became fully acclimated to war. I told myself, *Death in combat is a fact of life.* From time to time, the enemy would rush our perimeter, like hunters looking for the best shots. Our troops waited for them to come close, almost until they could see the whites of their eyes in the moonlight, then they'd knock 'em off one after another. Some enemy fell within ten feet of our perimeter. Their mortars kept coming, each round throwing dirt sky high. When one landed close, the blast would pick me up and throw me to the ground. Dazed and with ears ringing, I'd make it over to another wounded.

One guy had taken a lot of shrapnel in both legs. Litter-bearers helped me pull him to the middle of our formation for protection. The litter guys put tourniquets high on his thighs to help stop the bleeding. I gave the soldier a shot of morphine and dressed his wounds. As I turned to crawl back to my area, I heard, "Doc, I'm hit …it's Sarge!"

Sarge was one of our squad leaders. I crawled to him. He lay on his left side, holding his right arm. "Doc, I took a bullet to my arm. How's it look?"

"Lie still and take a deep breath. You'll be okay." There was just enough moonlight that I could see the bullet had traveled up his arm and lodged just below the elbow. I gave him morphine and wrapped a tourniquet high on his arm. I taped him up, put his arm in a sling, and tagged him WIA—wounded in action. The litter guys crawled over with a stretcher and put him in the middle of our formation with the other wounded until we could medevac. The enemy was within fifty yards and hitting us with everything they had.

I reached another soldier. He was moaning, his body full of shrapnel. He'd taken a direct hit. I knew right away he was going to die. His camouflaged helmet cover, ripped to shreds, lay beside him. I shot him up with morphine and cradled his head in my lap. He died within minutes. There was no time to mourn. I tagged him KIA and went off to find the next wounded soldier.

Our artillery arrived, along with two squads of troopers. Our artillery rounds pounded the enemy. Dead and wounded lay everywhere. Suddenly the enemy broke off the attack and ran back into the hills to their front line some three hundred yards away. Despite an all-out assault, the enemy had failed time after time to overrun our platoon. Their men lay shattered. We had inflicted maximum casualties on the enemy while minimizing our own.

We needed to medevac our seriously wounded. The Lieutenant called for two choppers. I told him our troops had fought with a lot of composure and guts for their first-ever patrol. Our first real experience in combat, and it was awful. I said, "If God ever created a hell-on-earth contest, Korea would make it to the finals."

"Amen!" said the Lieutenant.

The two choppers landed. Under cover of firepower, we flew out the wounded. Some two hours later we reached our MLR and gave the password, *iron*. The guard countered with *fist* and we crossed over the wire with our walking wounded. I stood on our MLR with the other medics and litter-bearers for a moment, looking out into the valley below where all the action had been. It was one night we wouldn't forget. This was one helluva way to spend my first full day in Korea. For me, it was the first step into hell.

Spool of communications ("commo") wire

CHAPTER 3

FIVE DAYS OF HELL

This was day five of our assault on a hill that was actually a mountain. The military called every mound of dirt and rock, no matter how tall, a hill. Our troops were in a brutal slugfest against the well-fortified Chinese Communist Forces, also known as the CCF. The assault had started up again on a cool 75-degree morning. I had not slept now for four days, except for a few catnaps, but then, who had?

The battle was furious, the terrain unforgiving. Our battalion had sent wave after wave of troops up the hill only to be met by every gun and mortar shell the Chinese had. It was like New Year's Eve. Our company, like the other three in the battalion, was taking one helluva beating. We had so many casualties that we set up a makeshift aid station in two big mortar craters behind a big knoll near the base of the hill. All around us, men were dying. We medics were working out in the open and bullets were flying. I wondered *would the next one have my name on it?* I wasn't the only medic who thought he wasn't going to make it.

There were literally thousands of Chinese shooting at us. The noise was deafening and unreal—ripping burp guns, blasting hand grenades, exploding mortars. My platoon had been pinned down for about twenty minutes when I heard a big blast to my right, then a cry of "Doc, Doc, over here!" I crawled up and over to where mortar shells had landed in a foxhole killing the two men there. A third soldier nearby had received the blast impact as well. "Hang in there and take a deep breath," I told him.

Cutting away the rest of his bloody fatigue pants, I saw his left leg was shattered, most of the flesh blown from the bone by shrapnel. Quickly I applied a tourniquet high on his thigh. Luckily, four of our litter-bearers were close by. The trooper was suffering from shock and had to be held down as I gave him a shot of morphine. I sprinkled sulfa powder on what was left of his leg and wrapped it up with four large battle dressings. Then I tied his leg to a splint the litter-bearers had. I tagged him as WIA and the litter-bearers carried him down the hill under a rain of bullets to our makeshift aid station.

As our troops moved up the hill, shells landed all around, throwing mud and debris sky high and back down on us. Following the troops, I found one dead Chinese lying alongside a foxhole, from a previous day because he was beginning to bloat. Flies and maggots were having a field day on the body. The smell was horrible. I rolled his body into the foxhole, used his rifle to push some dirt over him, stuck the point of the rifle into the ground and hung his helmet on the butt of the rifle. Any soldier passing by would know by this sign that a body was there.

A blast hit above me, sending chunks of shrapnel whizzing past. Sure as hell, debris hadn't even finished landing when I heard a cry of "Doc, Doc, my leg!" It was our platoon runner. "You'll be okay, I have everything under control," I said. But his right foot was nearly severed, blood everywhere. I had to move fast—yet under control.

I tied a tourniquet high on our runner's right thigh. His foot was still connected by part of the Achilles tendon, but otherwise cut cleanly off right at the boot top. I dusted it with a lot of sulfa powder and wrapped the damaged area of his leg with battle dressings. As I tagged him WIA, my litter-bearers appeared. They wrapped his boot with the foot in it in a field jacket, keeping it close to the rest of the leg. I hoped and prayed the docs could re-attach it. I thanked the litter guys for their help and off they rushed through incoming mortar rounds and flying bullets. I found our radioman and had him call for a medevac chopper.

As we continued our way up the hill, a group of eight enemy came running down, firing at our guys and slashing with their bayonets. It was hand-to-hand combat. I hunkered down in a foxhole with my dagger in hand. When it was over, all eight Chinese were dead, and we had one dead and four badly wounded with slashed faces, arms, and legs. Their flak jackets had helped prevent main body wounds. No sooner had I finished patching the guys up when I heard a whistle and then an explosion. Our squad leader yelled, "Doc, get your ass down!" as a rain of mortar shells followed, leaving one helluva mess all around.

One of our troopers couldn't find a foxhole quick enough. He got sprayed with shrapnel and was in much pain. I gave him a shot of morphine and with the help of two litter-bearers we dragged him to a nearby shell crater. Rolling him onto his side, I told the litter-bearers to use my tweezers to work at pulling the two large pieces of shrapnel out of his buttock and I would work on his arm wounds. Small shrapnel pieces would wait until later. Using alcohol, I cleaned the arm wounds, then tore open two packets of small battle dressings to bandage him up. When the litter-bearers were done, I bandaged up the buttock wounds. I covered our trooper with one of the litter guys' field jackets, tagged him WIA, and put him face down on the stretcher for the long ride to the bottom of the hill. The trip would take some forty-five minutes or so.

Crawling from shell hole to shell hole, our platoon made it half way up the hill. Our troops were exhausted, but the hard part was still to come. Our platoon leader, the Lieutenant, or LT, said the other companies were making good headway up the hill as well. All companies were to hold their positions at the halfway point to wait for our artillery and big mortars to come and blast the hell out of the upper part of the hill for the final push to the top.

Chinese small arms fire kept on during the hour-long lull so we had to keep our butts down and be on the alert. I sent our litter-bearers down the hill to our makeshift aid station to re-stock my two aid kits with more morphine, tourniquets, sulfa, tape, gauze, alcohol, aspirin, Merthiolate antiseptic, battle dressings, and field medical tags. With a man watching over me with a big Browning Automatic Rifle, or BAR, I took forty winks. Forty winks only meant fifteen minutes because then the LT started yelling how the second half would be damn tough because of the terrain. This was the day we were going to the top, up the steep slope and over knolls and ridges, past caves and bunkers and a hundred shell craters.

Our barrage against the hilltop began, and when it stopped, our troops started their attack again, going over each cave, bunker, and hole they found remaining to flush out any Chinese left. Demolitions guys heaved satchel charges—bags of TNT—and other explosives into the Chinese positions. Some of our troops threw white phosphorus grenades as well, and our flamethrower guys were an additional measure. An enemy sniper hiding in one of the caves fired two shots, killing one of our troopers and wounding our squad leader. I rushed over, zigzagging all the way so as not to get hit by the sniper. The flamethrower guys charged up the hill to the sniper's cave and blasted it with napalm. Out ran the enemy screaming and covered in flames, falling to the ground a few yards out.

When I reached our squad leader, he was on the ground in a lot of pain. I cut open his bloody fatigue pants and saw the shot had gone clean through his right thigh. I tied on a tourniquet, then applied two battle dressings. I gave him one half grain of morphine, tagged him as WIA, and put him on a stretcher. By then, I was soaked in blood.

We had a ways to go yet to capture the hill. The enemy wasn't about to give up. A shell hit so close the concussion knocked me to the ground. When I came around, one of our platoon sergeants was looking down at me. "Doc, are you okay?" I could barely hear him and thought my eardrums were broken. The ringing sound in my head was deafening. I looked myself over for blood—my own—but found no wounds. Our outfit had moved some one hundred yards up the hill. Sarge and I took off under small arms fire and made it up to our platoon.

As we got closer to the top of the hill, we saw where the shelling had taken its toll. Dead Chinese lay everywhere—in shell craters, caves, foxholes, and bunkers. LT told our troops that after four days of trying to take the hill and being pushed back, the fifth day was going to be the charm. "We owe it to the men we lost to take this hill. Let's go!"

I had to duck bullets and mortars to tend to our wounded and dying. From a distance came two very loud explosions. I waited a minute. Then one of our men yelled down the slope, "Doc, a mortar hit a foxhole and things don't look good!" When I got there, what a sordid scene. The shell had made a direct hit, killing our soldier taking cover in the hole. A trooper twenty yards away had his belly ripped open by the shrapnel. He was holding his intestines in his hands. If that wasn't bad enough, both his legs were torn up as well. I had to work fast. I gave him a big dose of morphine. He wanted water, but I said, "No way. Not with that stomach wound. Hang in there!"

Two of the litter-bearers held him as still as possible. I had two other litter-bearers put tourniquets high on each thigh to stop his legs from bleeding. Then I tried to put his intestines back in as best I could, but he grabbed my hand and died. I cut his dog tags off, putting one between his teeth and the other in my aid kit. I tagged the troopers as KIA and the litter-bearers put them on their stretchers for the ride down the hill and eventually to Graves Registration. A soldier passed me as I headed up the hill. "Doc, I wouldn't want your job."

"I did the best I could. May God rest his soul."

Then came another call for Doc. Three of our men had been found in an old mortar hole. Rigor mortis had set in. The bodies were covered with flies and maggots, their flak jackets gone. I tagged them as KIA and covered them with ponchos, then helped the litter-bearers tie them down on stretchers.

On the upper part of the hill our troops were still going at it strong. We had a few hours of daylight left. Sarge said we only had a few hundred yards to go before reaching the top. As we got closer, we saw more and more dead Chinese. Only a few rounds of firing went off here and there. It was just a matter of time. Then LT yelled down, "The hill is ours!" When we got to the top we couldn't believe our eyes. There had to be some five hundred to one thousand dead Chinese bodies—one helluva sight.

I spent most of the evening with the other medics patching up our wounded. Once we got all our wounded and dead down the hill, hours later, the battalion regrouped and began preparing for our next adventure in hell. But for now, our five days of this hell were over.

CHAPTER 4

SHADOWS OF DEATH

Our battalion came upon a valley known as "The Shadows of Death." Many had died trying to get through it, and steep hills around it cast huge shadows. It was a cool, late autumn afternoon. We were fighting our way northward. The going had been slow and bloody, costly for both sides. From the entrance of the valley, for as far as we could see, umpteen old burnt-out vehicles and destroyed tanks plus artillery and mortar rounds from past battles lay all around. In fact, everything that goes with war was scattered all over the valley between us and the enemy somewhere ahead. It looked like an old junkyard back home.

In the fall, darkness came early with the sun setting behind tall, rugged mountains. Soon the moon was shining between thick night clouds. Our battalion commander, the Colonel, sent one company at a time into the wide valley. Company A went first, then Company B. As Company C got about three hundred yards in, a storm of machine gun, burp gun, rifle, and mortar fire swept down on the whole valley from the hill to our left. Somehow over the noise we heard shouting for all companies to work their way over to the hill on our right. Mortar shells ripped the valley, the earth heaved, and bodies went flying.

My Company D made it about one hundred and fifty yards into

the valley. I jumped into a large shell hole and found the Lieutenant, our radioman, the interpreter, and our runner there. Company C's wounded and dead lay sprawled all around us. I heard calls for help, but the shelling was too much for me to go to the aid of the wounded. Since we weren't moving, I asked the Lieutenant if I and another medic could help Company C if we got the chance. "Okay, but Doc, don't get your asses shot off."

We waited until there was a moment's lull, then raced between the burnt-out vehicles and tanks. The whine of a mortar round sounded just as we started toward a cry for help. As we dove into a nearby shell hole, the mortar exploded some twenty yards away. I made a mad dash to a trooper lying out in the open and dragged him into our shell hole. He had been badly wounded. I applied a tourniquet, then took care of his arm wounds while my buddy medic patched up his leg. I gave the soldier a shot of morphine and tagged him as WIA.

Now came the hard part, getting the man back to our company some fifty yards away. We couldn't drag him that far in that terrain of junk and shell holes so I did the next best thing. I took the two aid kits on my web belt off and strapped them across the trooper's left shoulder. With the help of my buddy medic, we put the trooper over my right shoulder. It was going to be a tough go.

We heard another yell for help. I told my buddy, "Go for it, I'll be okay!" With shells landing all around and bullets zinging over our heads, I made a run for it. I stopped behind a burnt-out tank for cover and a minute of rest and yelled to the Lieutenant ahead to make room in the hole for the two of us and to radio for a stretcher. During the next lull in the shelling I ran over and dumped the trooper into our shell hole. I thought I was carrying an elephant! My weight was 175 at five feet ten inches. He weighed around 200 pounds and was about six feet. I don't know how I carried him, but I did.

By now it was really dark, but there were more wounded men to search for. I told the Lieutenant I was going back to help Company C and that I'd catch up with our platoon later. "Okay, Doc, stay low."

I was in a shell hole crouched over a wounded giving him aid. Next thing I knew, I was lying on my back, stunned. A corporal yelled, "That mortar round blew you three feet in the air!" I was unhurt, just a tad wobbly. I took an aspirin and finished patching up the wounded soldier.

My company was still pinned down by heavy mortar fire, but the other companies had reached the bottom of the hill to our right. The shelling stopped, but the machine gun, burp gun, and small arms fire kept on. Now was our chance to make our move. Inch by inch our company fought their way past the burnt-out tanks, trucks, and weapons carriers. We medics went from shell hole to shell hole patching up the wounded, listening to enemy fire.

After some eight hours of heroic fighting, our company made it to the rendezvous area at the bottom of the hill, but at a cost of ten dead and twenty-five wounded. Bullets ricocheted across the tops of the broken tanks and vehicles in the valley below. Time and time again, Company C tried to move forward to attack, hiding behind the junk in the valley. Time and time again, they were driven back. The fighting was vicious and bloody every step of the way.

We still had wounded in the valley that needed help. Plans were for the battalion to assault the enemy hill at 0300 hours, giving us medics an hour and a half to get our wounded and dead out of the valley. We set up a makeshift aid station behind a huge boulder about fifty yards up our hill. In the darkness, we moved slowly in every direction, listening for cries for "Doc."

I came upon a soldier who had crawled under a burnt-out tank. He'd been hit by machine gun fire in both legs and had lost a lot of blood. We had to get him out fast. I gave the trooper a shot of morphine. Litter-bearers arrived to help. In the dark, finding a vein to give him blood plasma was the hard part, so one of the litter guys held my small penlight and his buddy held a towel to hide the light from the enemy. Once the plasma was going, the litter-bearers carried the trooper out on the stretcher, with me zigzagging alongside, one hand holding the needle in the trooper's arm, the other holding the bottle of plasma up. Bullets ricocheted around us. We made it to our aid station behind the rock.

As the fighting calmed down, all companies quietly moved down our hill and into the valley to ready for the assault on the enemy. The signal to attack would bring an all-out artillery and mortar barrage. At zero hour all hell broke loose. A ten-minute rain of artillery and mortar rounds lit up the top of the enemy's hill. I didn't see how any animal, much less any human being, could live under that enormous barrage.

Our companies hit the hill. The terrain was rugged. Our troops poured automatic weapons fire and grenades on every position they came upon. Five or six Chinese came charging down at our platoon only to be stopped by a buzz saw of automatic weapons. The only escape route the enemy had was down the backside of their hill.

We took our share of wounded and dead. I had already patched up fifteen to twenty badly wounded. Our flamethrower guys leapfrogged up and down trenches and bunkers burning the enemy out. As I made my way up through a gully, a deafening storm of mortar shells hit the midsection of the hill. Frightened Chinese fled from their trenches. The fighting continued for what seemed like hours.

As I approached the top of a knoll, the zing of bullets sounded over my head. I heard the moaning and crying of a wounded. I could barely make out the dark figure lying on the hillside. He had been shot at close range by burp gun fire. Lying a few yards away was a dead Chinese soldier, his burp gun beside him. "Hang in there, you'll be okay," I told the trooper. I yelled for my buddy medic to hop to it, and within minutes he showed up. I cut open the trooper's fatigues. He had six bullet wounds. Two to his left leg, three to his right, one to his hand. We stopped the bleeding and as my buddy medic put on the last of numerous bandages, I gave a shot of morphine. The soldier was going into a mild case of shock. I yelled for the litter-bearers and told them to rush him to the aid station we had set up at the base of the hill. I tagged the soldier WIA and wrote on the tag to recommend him for a Bronze Star for courageous action. The boy was seventeen and his birthday was next month. I told him he might be home in the States in time for the party.

Daylight was just around the corner. The moon had disappeared, but it was still dark. Our platoon zigzagged their way to about two-thirds up the hill. We found hundreds of burnt Chinese bodies. Most had died from the white phosphorus of our shelling. As our Lieutenant said, "War sure is hell."

But it wasn't over yet. We still had a ways to go before reaching the hilltop. Our area had been under sporadic mortar fire. Throughout the early morning hours, the Chinese defenders fought stubbornly. Suddenly a shell landed about fifty yards from us. I ducked into a hole, but one of our litter guys got hit in the arm as he threw himself on the open ground. I crawled over to him, shells bursting around us. As each landed, the explosion kicked up dirt sky high. With each shelling we thought it'd be our last day on earth. After four or five interminable minutes, the shelling stopped.

The litter-bearer crawled with me to a shell hole. I took off his flak jacket. A jagged piece of shrapnel, about two to three inches long, stuck out of his upper left arm. How far into his arm it went, I didn't know, but I had to get it out. I stopped the bleeding with a tourniquet, then gave a shot of morphine. I swabbed the area with Mercurochrome. *Here goes.*

I used a small knife to cut out the shrapnel as carefully as I could—it's important for medics to stay calm under fire. After bandaging the man, I wrote on his tag that he needed a tetanus shot. I marked him as WIA, put his arm in a sling, and had him walk down the hill with his buddy litter-bearer to our makeshift aid station. As he was working his way down, he yelled back, "Doc, I owe you a beer!"

The shelling and gunfire stopped as suddenly as it had begun. The Chinese must have decided the hill was not worth the cost of more lives. In the early morning darkness, they withdrew what troops remained and left the hill in our hands.

The whole top of the hill was littered with dead Chinese, many stacked four to five high. I'd say there were an easy five hundred or more of them. It had been a vicious struggle all the way for us. Every soldier who fought in that day's battle would surely never forget it. People the world over need to know that war is hell on earth.

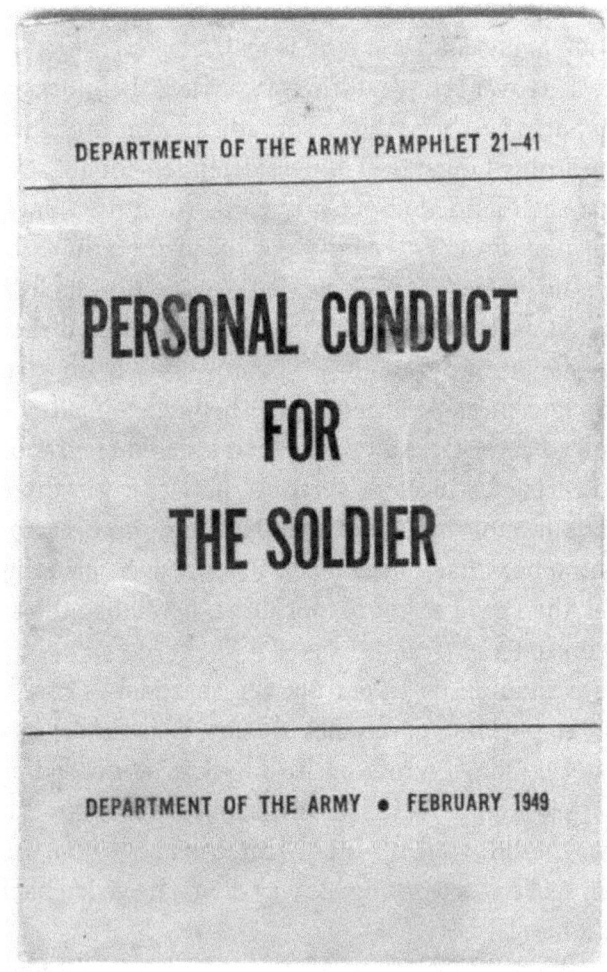

CHAPTER 5

TILL HELL FREEZES OVER

We were on our third day of fighting a Chinese force of 100,000. Our battalion of four companies totaled only 1,050 men. We were on a hill we had just taken four weeks ago, and the enemy wanted it back. They had to get past our minefields on the slope, then go some two hundred yards up to reach our trenches. They launched assault after assault as they tried to overrun us with their manpower. Every assault made our small defense that much weaker. More and more of our men were dying, partly because we medics couldn't keep up with all the wounded.

This time, both sides had another enemy—the weather. It had been drizzling off and on since the day before. Big black clouds were rolling down the valley toward us. The cold rain became a freezing rain. The temperature dropped to 28. Things did not look good. The air got colder by the hour. The wind blew from the north, directly into the faces of our trench line troops. We did our best to ignore the bitter cold and the freezing rain that intermittently swirled in the air. The Chinese kept coming up our hill in wave after wave. One of our line troops said, "This is a frozen hell on earth," as I made my way down the trench toward a call for "Doc" from Area 4.

Blood soaked the snow around the wounded trooper. I knelt down and saw he had three bullet holes to his chest. He was not wearing his bulletproof vest. Why? I do not know. Everyone else had theirs on. He whispered, "Would you tell my mom how it happened?" I said, "When I write to her I'm going to tell her you were a hero." He slumped over in the snow. I tagged him KIA, put one of his dog tags between his teeth and the other in my aid kit, then covered him up. The litter-bearers would pick him up later.

Word came down that one of our platoon sergeants was badly wounded. I headed to Area 2. Bullets zipped overhead. The sergeant was lying in the snow-covered trench. He had taken a bullet to his right shoulder. After putting the sergeant's right arm in a sling, the litter-bearers took him off to our medical bunker on the back slope. The medics there would give him more care. The sergeant's squad leader had taken over his position with the BAR. As I left, he was blasting away down the hill at the oncoming Chinese.

I and probably every soldier on the hill were utterly miserable, from both the cold and the fighting. The Chinese laid down another mortar barrage and more machine gun fire. Making my way down the trench line, I saw more attacking troops ahead of me. Our platoon leader, the Lieutenant, had set up a stronger offensive perimeter on our sector of the hill after a few Chinese had penetrated and killed six of our men before being gunned down. Our machine gunners hammered away at the hundreds of Chinese making their way up our hill. The Lieutenant called in the big guns. During the hour-long artillery barrage, an estimated 2,600 rounds fell on the oncoming enemy.

By 1200 hours the temperature had plummeted to the single digits—nine degrees below zero—and dismal Siberian winds whipped down from the north, pounding us with snow. Some of the troops were frostbitten. At times I couldn't put a needle in the arms or legs of the wounded—their skin was frozen. Our litter-bearers helped bring some of the frostbitten men to our heated rear bunkers on the back slopes.

I made my way up through the snowy trenches to Area 3. Bullets were flying. A trooper yelled that his rifle had failed in the cold. The plummeting temperature was then 18 degrees below zero. The trooper needed another weapon fast, and said his and his buddies' C-rations were frozen solid as well. Within minutes our squad leader brought the line trooper another weapon. I told him I'd get more C-rations for them once things calmed down. They weren't so good anyway, probably leftovers from WWII, like a lot of our equipment.

Mortars rained down again. I got as low as I could in the snowy trench. Now shrapnel as well as bullets zinged overhead. Suddenly it all stopped and I could hear the cries of "Doc!" everywhere. I ran along the trench line to Area 2 where the calls seemed loudest. A trooper yelled, "Up here, Doc!" With bullets flying again, I climbed my way up out of the trench. Two troopers were lying in the snow. One said, "Him first, over there."

I crawled in the snow to where he pointed, about fifteen feet away. When I reached the soldier, I found part of the back of his head missing. His helmet lay ten feet away. I felt for the carotid artery on either side of his throat. *He's not going to make it. It's only a matter of time.* I remembered the rule, no shots for head injuries since morphine would make the wounded even more disoriented so he couldn't tell me how he was doing. I gave the trooper a shot anyway for the pain. "Lie still," I told him, "Really still." Lucky it was damn cold. That helped to lessen the bleeding. I wrapped two large battle dressings around his head to hold together what was left, then laid him across my lap. His head rolled to one side and he was gone. I tagged him KIA and the litter-bearers took him to our rear aid station on the back slopes. I went to tend to the other trooper.

By midafternoon it was still snowing, and growing colder by the minute. We were getting hit hard by enemy fire. I made my way back to our medical aid bunker. Our wounded were piling up at an alarming rate. In the bunker were five or six of our trench line troops with their feet frozen, some so badly that I knew they'd lose one or more toes or even a foot. Others would lose one or more fingers.

After refilling my two aid kits, I left the bunker for Area 3 and ran into our squad leader. He said word had come down from our

Command Post bunker that there was a noticeable difference in the size of the Chinese force in their last assault wave. Since we had lost a lot of our men due to frostbite or being wounded or killed, the CP said to tell our sector of the hill that all line troops were to move up and down the trenches, to fire from different positions to give the impression that we were still fully manned. We still had to fight off the Siberian winds, the snow, and the frigid cold. It was hell on that hill.

As I left for Area 1, I heard the screams of "Doc! Doc!" everywhere. When I finally made it there, I found three dead soldiers lying in the snow-filled trench. Above the trench, a voice called, "Doc, up here." As bullets flew overhead from all directions, I made my way topside and crawled over to the nearest soldier. "What in the hell happened here?"

A mortar shell had gotten the three men. The trooper said he and his buddy had crawled out of the trench. They were hit by a grenade as the Chinese tried to overrun their position. Lying in the snow about ten feet away were three dead Chinese he said he'd killed with a burp gun taken from the enemy. He wasn't wounded too badly. He pointed, "My buddy is somewhere over there. Look at him first." I said, "Cover me."

I crawled to where he pointed. Blood covered the whole area. I found the soldier, the fatigue pants on his left leg ripped. He had suffered numerous wounds. I quickly put a tourniquet high on his left thigh. With the help of his buddy, we got him to the safety of our trench. He had a lacerated femoral artery. I couldn't help him. He was going fast. His buddy said, "Luck's not on his side."

While his buddy covered us with the burp gun, I knelt down beside the dying soldier and held his hand. It was cold and wet. He squeezed my hand and whispered, "Doc…thanks for giving it the old college try…Give 'em hell." When the litter-bearers arrived, I told them to tag him KIA. They would do the same to the three dead in the trench.

I crawled over to the soldier with the burp gun. He was lucky. He had only taken some shrapnel to the left side of his face and left arm. Nothing serious. After tending to him, I tagged him WIA. He went back to his front line position to continue firing away at the oncoming Chinese.

The sun had gone down and snow was coming down even harder. We already had eighteen inches of the white stuff and the temperature now was at 21 below zero. Then we heard the blowing of bugles in the distance. Just as suddenly as the fighting had started some two and a half days ago, the enemy shelling stopped. Their troops retreated down our hill.

Word then came down from our Lieutenant to cease firing. Hundreds, if not thousands, of frozen bodies lay on the snow-covered ground in front of us. Many had died in artillery barrages before they'd even had a chance to fight. As far as we could see with the moon shining on the snow, hundreds of Chinese troops were fading into the hills across the valley, withdrawing to lick their wounds and count their losses. After days of non-stop action, the Chinese knew they had been in one helluva fight. One thing for sure, we were going to hold that hill till hell froze over.

Library of Congress, Prints and Photographs Division

CHAPTER 6

PITCHFORKS AND BROOMSTICKS

On this bone chilling, 18-below-zero day in Korea, four inches of snow lay on the ground. Word had come from higher up that sometime tonight we could expect a massive attack in our sector of the front lines. Who would want to fight in such cold? The Chinese, that's who. And by attacking us in the dark, they could avoid our air power. This would be the first fight for our new replacements of two weeks ago. They would hear the clamor of the horns, bugles, drums, and whistles. Maybe they would see the hundreds of old men and women, and often even children, sent to die.

We were well dug in and as ready as could be. We had an elaborate winding trench system, with plenty of supplies and ammunition. And, we had one big advantage—our bunkers were heated with charcoal or oil-burning stoves. They weren't all that warm, but anything helped. Our line troops had to remember, though, that the Chinese were tough, vicious fighters who fought hard under any kind of condition and often attacked without regard for their own casualties.

I had just made my rounds in the trenches to see how our troops were holding up in the cold night when the moment of truth arrived. As gunfire echoed in the valley below, the brilliant glare of our flares revealed the Chinese enemy. Thousands were swarming into the valley in an all-out drive to overwhelm us. They had about five football field lengths of steep terrain to climb and hundreds of mines and booby traps to come through before they could reach our MLR. Sporadic phosphorous shells came at us, but they were not near enough yet to be a peril.

Our sector of the MLR was divided into four platoons, each with a color code—red, white, blue, or green. Each platoon was then divided to cover four trench areas. The wounded could yell out their platoon color and trench area and we medics and litter-bearers would know where to find them. If things got bad, we could go help out another color and area. Eight medics and sixteen litter-bearers were with each platoon. My assignment was Green Four. As I headed there, in came a mortar barrage and we all took cover. In a few minutes, it was over and I heard yelling from the Red and Blue areas. Then we heard the clamor of horns, bugles, and whistles and the sound of drums beating. I knew what was coming next.

Our white flares again shot up, lighting the whole valley floor and beyond. The Chinese were coming, yelling and screaming and holding their weapons high. Looking through night field glasses, our Lieutenant saw these weren't the Chinese troops, they were old men, women, and children. They were carrying pitchforks and broomsticks over their heads. These folks and the children were being sent up to be blown to pieces, clearing the ground of the mines and booby-traps we had set for the oncoming enemy troops. They wouldn't have a chance. If that wasn't enough, most did not have gloves, hats, or coats, and most wore tennis shoes, no boots.

Our replacement troops couldn't believe what they were seeing. I told them the Chinese were ruthless. "Don't let your guard down for one moment!" We had to spray them with machine gun fire. The Chinese sometimes made the civilians carry grenades, even the little kids. If they tried to turn around or run away, the Chinese would shoot them. The Chinese troops came up next, controlling their strong thrust against us, probing for weak spots in our sector. This was the pattern of fighting for the next several hours. The enemy attacked in overwhelming numbers.

Nearing midnight and now 20 below zero, the barrels of some of our machine guns glowed red and were beginning to sag from the heat of constant firing. They had to be replaced immediately as to not miss a beat. We were taking our share of casualties. The Lieutenant yelled from time to time for his troops to hold their fire until the enemy got within 130 meters so as not to waste ammo. With a fairly clear line of fire almost always available to our troops, at times it was like a turkey shoot. Bright bursts of light were followed by howls and screams, then moments of silence.

The Lieutenant rotated his men to warm bunkers every chance he could. While I patched up our wounded in one of our bunkers, a buddy medic asked me if I knew I had three bullets stuck in my bulletproof vest. I had been knocked down a couple of times, but didn't know what had hit me. He said, "You don't have to be a church-going person to know there's someone looking over you."

I went back to Green Four to bring in one of the line troops who had two frostbitten fingers. On the way to the medical bunker, the trooper said the cold had made many of our carbines and some of the pistols unusable. The big BARs, however, were resisting freeze-up. As I left the medical bunker again, someone yelled, "Doc, Blue Three!" Their medic needed help. One of our machine gunners had taken a bullet to his left forearm. I knocked the snow off his fatigues and cut the sleeve open to the shoulder, then put a tourniquet above the gunner's elbow. Lucky for him the bullet had hit the fleshy part of his forearm and gone through. I took care of the wound and tagged him WIA.

I returned to Green Four and was giving aid to one of the troops when I noticed a Chinese soldier had crawled up to our trenches. He had made it through our minefield and the barrage of shooting. As he stood to aim his weapon, one of our sharpshooters fired a single shot that tore through the man's chest. I was only a few feet away as he fell backwards onto the snow-covered ground. The soldier's face showed no sign of pain or agony, only the grim, empty look of death.

Artillery shells exploded all around. The Chinese dead were stacked like cordwood. What a scene of carnage. The lonely, agonized moans of the wounded could be heard as they lay dying.

At 0200 hours the fire on both sides was still murderous. Neither snow nor cold nor darkness slowed the fighting. The Chinese attacked time and time again, and each time were beaten back. We up on the hill had the advantage—as the enemy struggled to climb up to us, we picked them off. They crawled over heaps of their own dead and wounded. Our battle-tired and half-frozen men cut them down with sharp bursts from their machine guns, dropping the enemy by the hundreds. They knew they were being slaughtered, but some still crept, clawed, and fought their way up the steep terrain of our hill to meet their end.

Artillery shells from both sides lit up the dark sky. I made my way down the trench toward another call for "Doc," shells blasting all around. I found one of our platoon squad leaders lying in the snow. Beside him, dead, was our platoon runner. Both had been hit by shell fragments. Our squad leader was holding onto his intestines.

"Hang in there!" I told him. "Try not to talk." I yelled for the litter-bearers. I needed to get the man into a heated bunker fast. I didn't tell him things didn't look good. Large shell fragments had torn one helluva hole right into his abdomen. My hands were numb with cold as I held his intestines and carefully pushed them back into his body. The litter-guys arrived within minutes and we put our squad leader onto the stretcher. I put large battle dressings to the trooper's abdomen and held them on as I walked alongside the litter-bearers carrying him to the medical bunker. It was a slow go, with a hailstorm of bullets whistled over our heads. On the way, he grabbed my hand. "Doc . . . I know stomach wounds are a slow death." About ten yards from our bunker, his hand dropped from mine. I tagged him KIA.

After restocking my aid kits, I headed back down the trench, dodging bullets to get to Green Four. Our litter-guys were carrying dozens of frostbitten line troops to treatment at our battalion aid station. Just as I got to the MLR, our battalion artillery and large mortar shells hit the enemy in the valley below with a double whammy of fire. Our superior firepower dealt out severe punishment. I figured that when daylight hit—in about two hours—we could destroy the rest of the enemy. Then came the sound of a bugle blowing. Our flares went up, and we saw hundreds of Chinese troops in the valley floor below retreating as fast as they could.

"Hold your fire," yelled the Lieutenant. "It's all over for now, but in a few days, they'll be back."

I headed to my medical bunker to help with the wounded and frostbite cases. I was sure our new replacements would always remember this battle and the pitchforks and broomsticks that came first.

CHAPTER 7

JITTERY AND JUMPY

Word had come down from Intelligence that a large-scale Chinese attack was believed imminent. When and where remained a matter of conjecture, but HQ thought our sectors might be the ones hit by the CCF. Scuttlebutt had it the force was 270,000 or more. Their objective was probably the 3,890-foot-high mountain in our area of the MLR. Things were relatively quiet this February evening. Snow had been falling all day, half a foot so far, and the temperature was 27 degrees below zero.

Our CO, a captain, held a meeting of all platoon leaders as well as all medics and litter-bearers. We were to prepare for the worst. "Fix bayonets" was the order of the day. The troops were to get ready for one helluva fight. In my mind I could see the enemy coming across our MLR in droves. We figured we had a little over five hours to prepare. As the evening went on, the wind increased and the temperature dropped. We had heard that at times during North Korean winters the ground could be frozen hard as a rock, with temperatures down to 50 degrees below zero. That's cold!

It was a perfect night for the enemy to attack—no moonlight. I was as jittery and jumpy as a jackrabbit, but I told our troopers things would be A-OK. This would not be the first time the Chinese had attacked our MLR in huge numbers. Not long ago, an estimated

350,000 or more hit our lines in a battle that lasted some ten hours. Each time, our troops pushed them back, but at a great loss of men. This would be the first big battle, however, for many of the fresh troops that had been brought in to help replenish the battalion, and it scared the hell out of them.

I went up and down the trenches and bunkers to see if any of the troops needed anything medically. I shot the bull with them, trying to relax them, calm them down and boost their morale for what was coming. Was I scared? *Damn right I was scared!* But I couldn't let the troops see that. Anyone who has faced combat and tells you he wasn't scared is lying. Our young soldiers worried and asked me, "Am I going to die? Doc, I don't have much time, do I." I tried to encourage them. General Dwight D. Eisenhower once said, "Morale is the greatest single factor in successful wars."

For men who had been in war a while, sometimes combat fatigue took its toll. In training I was told everyone has what's called "the breaking point," and it varies with the individual. The stress of combat, especially if day in and day out, can be overwhelming to the point where some guys just plain give up. Some got shell-shocked. Fear would set in and then came sobbing and feelings of helplessness. In World War II that was called "Section 8." Some thought of killing themselves, thinking they weren't going to make it out alive anyway. The fear and uncertainty were just too much. A few went to the extreme of shooting themselves in the foot or leg to try to get sent home. People who have never witnessed war firsthand have no idea what war can do to a person. There's a reason combat veterans keep saying war is hell.

On my rounds I handed out pills and foot powder. I was always running out of foot powder to keep the troopers' feet dry. Two things worried me the most about the extreme cold—trench foot and frostbite, both caused by prolonged exposure to cold and moisture. The first stage is pale skin and pain. If the condition wasn't treated, gangrene could set in, then amputation might be necessary. Keeping their feet dry was a real problem for front line troops. Everyone wore big thermal Donald Duck boots with two pairs of thick wool socks. On the front line, many men never changed clothes except for their socks. I tried like hell to have them change socks every day or every other day. The socks they put on weren't clean, but at least they were dry. Frozen feet were my worse fear. I knew troops who had lost toes or an entire foot. I told them if they kept their feet dry and powdered, cold wasn't as dangerous. Some would listen to me, some wouldn't. What was a medic to do?

I had a plan in place. When not in battle, I'd rotate every other line trooper to his bunker. They were to take their thermal boots off and switch socks, right to left, left to right. While one sock was off, the trooper was to dry his foot, rub his toes for five minutes, and then powder the foot. This wasn't the daily routine for the average front line trooper because some battles would go on for days, even weeks at a time. A soldier was lucky just to stay alive, but I gave it my best effort to prevent frostbite. That's what counts.

Luckily, I had gone down to the battalion aid station two days ago to fill my aid kits and resupply our medical bunker. I had also picked up medicine and equipment for the other medics and litter-bearers. While making my rounds I noticed the explosives experts checking the booby traps and flares in the minefields in front of our position. Our minefield went down as far as the valley below, some five hundred to eight hundred yards in front of our MLR. The enemy would have to come up through all of that to get to us.

We medics worked out a system to handle the wounded and dead, knowing we wouldn't have our choppers because of the heavy firefight that was about to ensue. Each company would put their dead in one of the back slope bunkers. The badly wounded and the men with frostbite would go in one of the back heated bunkers with a medic to care for them. Each bunker would have a trooper guarding it. If there was a lull in the action, the litter-bearers would take the wounded down the hill to a waiting litter jeep. The jeep would then take them to the battalion aid station about five hundred yards behind our MLR.

We were still short of men. We were down to sixteen medics from twenty-four a week ago. Down to twenty-four litter-bearers from thirty-two. This to cover all four companies in the battalion. Every outfit up and down our front line was short of medics because the enemy was killing them—they hoped that would hurt the spirits of our troops. We medics were glad to be wearing some new-issue bulletproof vests. I'd have my work cut out for me, covering some 150 yards of trench line. It would be a rough go with the cold and snow and all, but we were dug into fixed position, the trenches giving us some cover. Trenches were about four feet wide and shoulder or head high. At least we were more or less not out in the open, except when we had to climb out to rescue a wounded.

The temperature had dropped to 37 below zero, making it a problem for anything mechanical to function properly. A light snow was still falling. We all had our heavy clothing, but that didn't help much. It was the coldest I'd ever felt in my life. We were all freezing our butts off, and that was putting it mildly. I had told our troops to wear their mittens. Military mittens were made so the men could still use their weapons—the trigger finger as well as the thumb were separate. Mittens were better than gloves because heat would transfer between adjacent fingers. As a medic, I often had to go without hand protection so I could do my job.

If the extreme cold was hard on our troops, it was hard on the enemy as well. Many of the Chinese lacked adequate warm clothing. Their equipment broke down. Water froze in the boilers of their train engines. Oil froze in their trucks. Grease froze in their guns. Their machine guns would freeze up. We had our problems with equipment, too, but we cleaned our weapons after every battle or even during lulls in fighting. We rubbed in cosmoline oil, which was like putty and stunk like hell. The partially-mechanized Chinese army had to find horses to hitch to their tanks and trucks that would break down or freeze up. They'd even use old farm wagons to cart their supplies. Wounded Chinese foot soldiers often died where they fell—not from their injuries, but from shock and frostbite.

There was really no way we could prepare for what was coming. We did the best we could under the circumstances. We knew some of the enemy would get through, but how many? In our thinking, the valley below would be a death trap. We held the high ground and had the whole valley zeroed in. We'd shoot up an occasional flare that would burst and parachute down, lighting up the area in front of us to reveal any enemy trying to get through. Our battle plans had been mapped out ahead of time. We were ready to call in our mortars and artillery when needed, giving them coordinates to any target.

At midnight the whole MLR was on red alert. We didn't have to wait any longer. True to form, in the darkness of night we heard the cacophony of yells. Then came the sound of troops rushing up our mountain. They hit our lines with everything they had, kitchen sink and all. Mortars and artillery rounds by the hundreds came in on us, followed by the enemy's usual bugle- and whistleblowing and drum-banging tactics. That was followed by human waves of attack. They stormed up the hill by the thousands. While our division and battalion hurled salvo after salvo into the Chinese assembly area below, many shell rounds fell within seventy-five yards of our front line, killing hundreds of Chinese troops. They were also met by our eight machine guns and by our line troops firing automatic weapons, BARs, and burp guns. Our mines and booby traps blew up all over the place.

We shot flares up from time to time, and in the light we saw piles of Chinese bodies below us on the forward slopes of the hill. After two hours, enemy forces were still pushing through the artillery and mortars of both sides. Some of the enemy had gotten through our defensive positions and were engaging our troops in close hand-to-hand combat. Screams, some like the blood-chilling howl of wolves, came from up and down our trenches, followed by calls of "Doc, Doc, I'm hit!"

As I answered cry after cry, shells from both sides landed everywhere around me—in front, behind, and in the trenches. My hands by now were freezing and numb. From time to time I'd put them between my legs a minute to warm them, but that didn't really help. With litter-bearers beside me, we made our way up the trench while automatic weapons fire buzzed overhead. We stumbled over dozens of dead Chinese. We found one of our machine gunners alive and in one helluva lot of pain, lying on top of some dead enemy. His assistant gunner had taken over his position and was firing away at the oncoming Chinese. He said, "Doc, he was just hit, and hit bad!"

One of the litter-bearers held my penlight, using a tarp to hide the shine from the enemy, and the other had his gun ready for any Chinese coming up or down the trench. I started peeling and cutting away the trooper's uniform. Why wasn't he wearing his flak jacket? Bullets had struck him in the chest, right shoulder, and right arm. He was soaked in blood. I tried to stop the flow of blood and the gurgling from a sucking chest wound, air pulling in through a bullet hole. We had to get him into the bunker behind us. Once there, one of the litter-bearers pulled blankets off some of the bunks and we wrapped the trooper up the best we could to warm him. I couldn't start an IV because even in the bunker the thing was frozen. If I didn't medevac the man fast, his chances were zilch, but the weather made it doubtful a chopper could get in. By now the snow was one foot deep and the temperature was 42 below zero. I prayed that God would spare the gunner's life, but it was just a matter of time. Whenever someone dies, as a medic you always ask yourself, *What could I have done differently?*

The battle raged on. With massed division artillery and mortar fire support, some 30,000 rounds fell on the area in front of our position. Heavy and accurate shelling prevented the Chinese troops below from making headway. We medics and litter-bearers aided some fifty to sixty or more of our wounded. The battle was as brutal as the harsh Korean winter. The smell of death and blood filled the air, mixing with the sharp scent of gunpowder. At about 0600 hours, the Chinese broke off the attack, suffering numerous more casualties as artillery raked their routes of withdrawal. By 0700 the situation was still not favorable for rapid cleanup as we could still hear a round or two coming from below our MLR, but for the most part the retreaters were across no man's land and back to their own front line.

We medics and the litter-bearers went up and down the snow-covered trenches in search of live bodies. At the entrance to one of our bunkers, I found six of our men dead and one still breathing. He had massive head wounds and a lot of damage from shrapnel. With the help of litter-bearers, we got him inside the bunker to get him warm. He was more or less out of it. I told him his ordeal was over and to hang in there, that I would do everything I could for him. After working on him for twenty minutes, I tagged him WIA. The litter-bearers took him back down our hill to the BAS for further treatment. Some of the troops told me they would prefer being blown apart to suffering the languishing agony of embedded shrapnel everywhere. A bayonet wound in the abdomen was bad, too, and everyone feared being left on the field alone to perish in torment from wounds or exposure to below zero weather. We would never leave anyone out there alive if we could find him, but we had to bury plenty of our dead out there because sometimes we couldn't carry them all back.

Many more solitary sufferers were discovered as we made our rounds. The frigid cold did save a few of the wounded from dying. If this had been the hot summer, they would have bled to death for sure. Instead it was so damn cold we had to run our litter jeep engines every fifteen minutes to keep them from freezing up. Evacuating our wounded was a problem. Once down the hill, our litter-bearers had a grueling half-mile walk through cold and a foot of snow to the battalion aid station.

Down the hill from our MLR, Chinese bodies were stacked one on top of another. We estimated thousands. Another three to four hundred lay in our trenches and bunker area, many killed by bayonet. On the other side of our hill lay another 150 or so enemy bodies. War is gruesome. The taste of triumph was in the air, but we all knew there would be other battles coming.

CHAPTER 8

DEATH, DEATH, EVERYWHERE DEATH

In Korea's winters only one thing happens: death from the frigid cold. It was 24 degrees below zero at 0900 hours and eight inches of snow had fallen. No matter how we dressed for it, even with our insulated rubber "Donald Duck" thermal boots, everyone suffered. We got up with the cold, we went to bed with it, and we couldn't escape from it.

Just twenty-four hours earlier, we had fought off a 500-man North Korean force. We wondered why they were in the Chinese area. Intelligence was working on that. From that battle, debris had been strung all over the place so our platoon leader, the Lieutenant, had the squad leaders get a detail to police-up our area of the MLR. Yes, in all that cold we had to clean up the mess. Abandoned weapons, empty ammo boxes, ammunition of all kinds, shell casings, blown-up mortar shells, canteens, medical dressings, empty syringes, etcetera, plus dead gooks by the dozens lay everywhere. Enemy bodies would be bulldozed into mass graves, but any live ones would be taken to G2 for interrogation. If we found any of our own dead, they'd be taken to Graves Registration. The Lieutenant and a special team of explosives experts reset our minefields, booby traps, and flares in the area in front of our MLR.

We were facing the Chinese Communist Forces, the CCF. Only 150 feet or so of no man's land lay between our trench line and theirs. We were eyeball to eyeball. We had to use caution in the daytime or be shot at by small arms fire. We, as well as the Chinese, patrolled almost daily, and both sides lost men during those patrols. Scuttlebutt from HQ had it that there was some rumbling, that our area of the MLR might again be hit tonight. Now we knew why the North Koreans had attacked us—to see how we would react and to soften us up for the Chinese. As a daily routine, our front line troops sharpened their bayonets and knives and checked all weapons to make certain they wouldn't jam when the time came to use them. We also made sure we had enough C-rations to last up to six days.

During the long wait to nightfall, the tension and frustration for some of the soldiers became almost unbearable. They were antsy, hyper-anxious, scared. Death lay in wait for them, but the flavor of life was strong. I could never let on that I was scared, too. I had to encourage the others. Whenever we got a brand new medic as a front line replacement, the first question he'd ask was "What's it like to see someone die right before your eyes?" I'd tell him be it the enemy or one of ours, it was not a happy scene. That is true even for an experienced combat medic like myself. But, it's something we have to face day in and day out on the battlefield.

In our jobs as combat medics, we look upon death as well as injuries of all kinds. To prepare the new medics, I'd tell them that when someone is dying it's like looking at a rag doll. Sometimes muscular spasms can draw up the whole body into a fetal position but then death starts to sink in and the body relaxes and grows limp and heavy. You tag the body and the litter-bearers take it to Graves Registration. You do not stop and think about it. You take a deep breath and move on to the next wounded.

I and another medic spent most of the day in the medical bunker picking out shrapnel and changing dressings on the arms and legs of men wounded in our last battle. As well, we aided those with frostbitten hands or feet, some developing gangrene. The other two medics made their way through the winding trenches, giving out pills, medicine, shots, etc. We had a few cases of soldiers who had fallen asleep and frozen to death at their posts. We had tagged them as KIA.

Darkness set into the hills and the temperature outside our aid bunker read 28 below zero. Bitter cold winds blew up to 25 miles per hour. The motor pool guys tried to start the vehicles' engines every hour or so to avoid having the engine blocks freeze up. We had already lost two medical aid jeeps to cracked blocks. The motor pool was always running out of antifreeze.

A few flares shot up here and there and small arms fire sounded in the distance. I was checking on aid supplies when our platoon leader called up on the sound power phone for all medics and litter-bearers to meet in his bunker. A sound power phone looks kind of like an old-style telephone but with a knob on the side that we cranked when we wanted to talk. One crank gave one ring, two cranks gave two rings, and the number of rings was a code for who the call was for, like for the CO or for our aid bunker.

Our platoon leader went over the schedule for our upcoming week's patrol and had just asked for an up-to-date medical report on the condition of his troopers when gunfire erupted. Artillery and mortar rounds came in like it was the Fourth of July in the USA. One of our forward observers phoned back to the CO from the outpost that all he could see through his night field glasses was a mass of Chinese soldiers in white clothing coming through no man's land. They covered the whole valley floor, blending in with the snow-white ground. He estimated the force to be about 25,000 or more. The CO sounded a red alert.

Ten minutes later the Chinese came swarming up our hill, blowing bugles and whistles, rattling tin cans, shooting off flares, and yelling and howling like a pack of coyotes. This time no horses, no armor, no vehicles. The Fourth of July turned into New Year's Eve. They shot their burp guns into the air, not at our troops on the front line. Many weren't wearing gloves despite the below zero cold. They had trouble holding their weapons. Ten inches of snow was already on the ground and flurries kept falling. It had to be a tough go for them to climb our hill.

Thousands of them came in waves toward our sector of the MLR. Our line troops killed them as fast as they came. When the first wave of about two thousand got halfway up our hill, incoming mail hit us. Most struck short of our MLR, landing in our minefields and on their own troops. Our units hurled salvo after salvo of outgoing mail over our heads, falling within fifty yards of our front line, killing hundreds more enemy. The night sky lit up, looking like day. The enemy's first wave faltered, then a second wave came, and then a third. With all the ammo flying around us, I was damn glad for my bulletproof vest.

Two hours went by and no let-up in sight. It was now close to midnight. We medics had been running all over the place attending to dozens of wounded and dead. The fight was taking a toll on all of us. I finished working on a badly wounded soldier and heard "Doc, I'm hit, Area 4!" On my way over, a blast went off nearby, like a hand grenade exploding.

When I got to Area 4, there was our platoon leader, the Lieutenant, leaning up against the wall of the trench, splattered in blood and snow, rifle by his side. Bullets from a burp gun had hit him in his right arm and right leg and the grenade must have exploded in his lap. I laid him down in the trench. He was trying to hold his intestines in. "Hang in there," I told him and ran down the trench a few yards to grab a fatigue jacket off a dead body. I used the jacket to cover the hole in the Lieutenant's stomach. "Thanks, Doc," he said, "I need water." I knew not to give water to someone with an abdominal wound, and I couldn't anyway because his canteen was frozen.

The Lieutenant was in one helluva lot of pain. I wanted to give him a shot of morphine, but I could tell he wasn't going to make it. I had only one syringe of morphine left tucked in the band of my helmet and heard more troopers yelling "Doc!" I had to make a judgment call. I chose not to give him the last of my morphine. I reached in my aid kit for a large battle dressing to cover the stomach wound. As I threw the bloody jacket aside, the Lieutenant looked up and whispered, "Doc, you're the best . . ." His eyes closed.

I yelled for the litter-bearers and tagged the body KIA, covering the Lieutenant with the bloody jacket. Off I went toward another cry for "Doc," but looked up to see one of our front line troopers had been hit by a sniper. With one of our BAR guys covering me, I jumped up and over the trench and crawled out about ten feet to the wounded man. Bullets rang past my helmet, others kicked up the snow in front of me. The soldier told me the shot had spun him completely around. He had a terrific burning feeling, like a hot poker, going through him. I thought maybe the bullet had hit his ribcage and gone through his lungs. I knew one thing—he'd been hit and hit bad. I was glad that I had saved that one last syringe of morphine. I gave him the shot and patched him up the best I could under the conditions, just to keep him alive. We had to get him out fast. One of our squad leaders yelled over that he had a litter waiting. I dragged the soldier back to our front line, two of our BAR men blasting away over me with their powerful rifles. It was a slow go, taking ten minutes to get him the ten feet or so back to our MLR.

We had no idea what was happening over on the other side of the mountain. Scuttlebutt had it our other companies were getting the shit kicked out of them. Another handful of enemy made it through our lines and were discovered hiding in one of our food bunkers. They were killed on the spot. It was now 0100 hours and the temperature was minus 31 degrees below zero. Things were bad, really bad. We had dozens of soldiers with hands and feet frostbitten. We tagged them all as having "frozen extremities" and sent them down our back slope to the aid station. I myself was frozen, dirty, and exhausted. My hands had turned purple. I was simply trying to stay alive, like everyone else on the hill. I had learned one thing as a combat medic, though—never to panic, stay calm in a chaotic situation. *Things are going to be okay,* I told myself. *Take a deep breath and move on.*

The Chinese were really taking a beating. If we had it bad, they had it much worse. The fighting went on for another hour and a half.

Then faster than they had come, those that had survived retreated, carrying their wounded with them. Our snowy trenches were filled with hundreds of dead enemy. We had plenty of wounded and dead of our own. My own clothes and exposed skin were covered in cold, dried blood and I could not escape the smell. To this day I will never forget the smell of death. Nor, I'm sure, will the men who survived. As one of my buddy medics said: Death, death…everywhere death.

CHAPTER 9

BOOT PRINTS IN THE SNOW

There were times when I really felt sorry for our front line troops. This was one of those days. At 0600 hours, the temperature was zero degrees. The troops in the trenches were freezing their butts off, and putting up with that raw, frigid wind coming from the north. No matter how much clothing they wore, that wind still penetrated to their bones.

It's the front line soldier who takes it to the enemy. It is he who goes face to face, toe to toe with the enemy, with rifle and with bayonet. It is he who fights to keep the small bit of real estate called the MLR. It is he who feels the ache and loneliness, the exhaustion and fear. It is he who, in my mind, is the bravest in the military.

The North Koreans had been pounding us the last five days. The weather had been fairly good—like 20 degrees above zero, not like today. Four medics covered our platoon's frontage of the MLR. We should have had another four medics, eight in all, but things had not been going well for us lately. The Chinese and the North Korean troops had been picking us off one by one while we gave aid to our wounded. So far I'd been damn lucky. I had been hit numerous times in my bulletproof vest by shrapnel and by bullets fired from a distance. If the bullets had been fired at close range it might have been a different story. The vest I was wearing was my third one. The other two had been torn to bits.

Our line troops were in the same fix us medics were in. They were short of men, but they were short of ammo as well. We combat medics were hoping new medics as well as more medical supplies would arrive soon. We were short of morphine, IVs, penicillin, alcohol pads, blood plasma, battle dressing, etc. As we made our morning rounds, we hoped this would be the day of delivery.

I went back to our medical aid bunker to resupply my aid kits. Incoming and outgoing rounds could be heard from time to time. The ground was covered with a foot of snow from two days ago. Scuttlebutt had it that something was in the making—what, no one knew. There was a lot of action coming out of the company command post bunker for the last day or so. The Captain called me on the sound power phone while I was in the medical aid bunker. "Doc, there's an ambush patrol planned for tonight, but now there's a problem. The medic down to go got banged up a bit. Would you go in his place? Sarge will be leading the patrol."

I told the Captain that I had gone on a few patrols with Sarge before and to count me in. I hoped we had enough ammo. Sometimes we'd get a gung-ho lieutenant who wanted to do a patrol or mission even though we didn't have enough guys or ammo. Then we'd be handed some bullets to "use sparingly." Once or twice I was able to persuade them not to go because we'd all get killed.

I went to the command post bunker to get the details from Sarge and the lieutenant in charge. The code name for the mission was *Operation Iceberg*. Six BAR men, four men with the enemy's burp guns and ammo, two sharpshooter riflemen with silencers, two rifle-grenade men, one radioman, one interpreter, Sarge, and me made for a total of eighteen men. Sarge had handpicked combat-seasoned men for the operation.

The Lieutenant told us, "All clothing will be white—white snowsuits, white boots, white mittens or white finger-gloves. All weapons will be white. Doc, your two aid kits will be white. All flak jackets will be white and are to be worn inside the snowsuits."

All on the patrol met at the forward bunker at 1700 hours (5:00 p.m.) to get instructions. Once through the wire, we would get orders by hand signals. We'd get into a small diamond formation. Every man knew his position. The radioman, the interpreter, and I would be in the middle. Our objective was to set up on a ridge overlooking a ravine that the North Koreans had taken when pulling off raids on our line troops. It was about a thousand yards out once we got through no man's land.

Sarge said, "We have to get there before they go through that area at around 2030 hours. Their raiding parties for the most part are always about fifteen to twenty men. Remember, no talking once through the wire. The password today is *Jack*, counter *Frost*." Sarge looked at his watch. "Time to move out."

It was a moonlit night, great for an ambush. Sarge had two BAR men behind us to guard our rear. They swept branches over our tracks to cover up our boot prints. Once we made it to the ridge, we got in a semicircle facing the potential gook patrol route below. I could see why it was a perfect site for an ambush. The ravine was narrow, about fifteen feet wide by some thirty feet long. It was packed with a foot of snow.

Lying there for an hour or so, I was hoping our men would remember to move their fingers and toes so as not to let them freeze. I moved my fingers inside my big white mittens and wiggled my toes in my white thermal Donald Duck boots. Those rubber boots were good if we stood still, but they'd make our feet sweat if we walked around too much, and then our damp feet would freeze. I remembered another patrol when it was 20 degrees below zero. We lay in the snow for four to five hours and had two soldiers who froze to death. I hoped we wouldn't repeat that scene again.

We heard loud voices and a lot of noise. We lay still, waiting for the North Koreans to walk into our ambush zone. Sarge gave the hand signal to be ready for action in one minute. He gave another hand signal to show there were twenty enemy. Once all twenty got into the ravine, our troops unleashed a fearsome volley of automatic weapons fire. Five enemy were killed instantly. The surviving North Koreans took cover the best they could. We had them pinned down for the moment. The fire from both sides lasted about ten minutes. Then all went silent. The enemy had gone to the right and left of us in the ravine. We could tell where they had gone by their boot prints in the snow.

Brief bursts of fire periodically came at us. Then up jumped two enemy brandished grenades. Before they could throw them, our two sharpshooters fired. Both gooks dropped out of sight into the ravine, moaning until the grenades exploded under them. That left thirteen to go. Suddenly the enemy let out a bunch of whooping and hollering. Two or three of them rushed up to our ridge, firing away and throwing grenades. Some fell and rolled back down on them, killing six of them. Shrapnel flew everywhere. A grenade landed near one of our BAR men and exploded. "Doc, I'm hit!"

I crawled about ten yards through the snow to reach our man. Shrapnel had ripped through his snowsuit, hitting him in the right arm and leg. I cut through his bloody suit with my dagger and put a tourniquet high on his arm and one high on his thigh. The bleeding stopped immediately—the cold weather helped. I didn't want him to go into shock. I gave him a shot of morphine for pain, then wrapped his arm and leg. With the biggest battlefield dressings I had, I wrapped the areas of his snowsuit that I had cut. I tagged him as WIA and asked the radioman to watch over him. "Release both tourniquets a little bit every five to eight minutes."

We had done away with thirteen enemy, leaving seven below us. Sarge yelled his orders. "Move in close to the edge of the ridge—I have a plan. Load up on grenades!" Sarge fired two white flares, lighting up the area. In the snow below, running like hell, were the remaining enemy trying to escape back down their path. Our men fired and threw their grenades, killing all seven. Sarge told us to pack up and get the hell out of there. He was thinking our ambush would bring on more enemy troops. As we went down the ridge heading home, half carrying our BAR man, I looked back. I saw our boot prints in the snow.

CHAPTER 10

EENY, MEENY, MINY, MOE

We had gotten the hell kicked out of us the previous two weeks by the North Koreans. They had hit us with a force of some 50,000 against our 1,500. Our battalion lost a total of twenty-two great guys, and had sixty-six wounded. Plus six had been captured. The company I was with had suffered most of the casualties, and my platoon had taken the worst beating—six dead and fifteen wounded.

One of our dead was a medic, my best buddy. My friend was shot in cold blood while working on a wounded. A sniper zeroed in and picked him off. Yes, he had the Red Cross on his helmet and on both armbands. The enemy could not have mistaken him for a combat soldier. The sniper got his just reward moments later, killed by one of our sharpshooters. I was the one who carried my friend off the battlefield and tagged him as KIA. That was a dark day in my life as a combat medic, but I had to go on. I was trained to move on. You have to put your soul on hold. There would be time later to think of the friends you lost and to tell their families the details they wanted to know.

We knew our company commander, the Captain, was planning a rescue mission to free the six soldiers who had been captured. Intelligence reports said they were in a small village behind enemy lines. The Captain had begun careful preparation two days ago for what might be the most arduous and daring venture for our company to date. He called me on our medical bunker sound power phone and asked if I'd meet with him in an hour, at noon. I had an idea what the meeting would be about.

I found a little crowd at the Captain's bunker. My platoon leader, the Lieutenant, was there as well as three other medics, one from each of the other platoons in our company. Sixteen guys I knew from the company were there, too. For the next hour and a half, the Captain went over the plan. The LT would lead the mission. The sixteen soldiers were all gung ho rarin' to go. They wanted to free their buddies. The Captain had to pick two out of us four medics to go on the mission. He went through the *Eeny, Meeny, Miny, Moe* jingle twice, like kids use to pick who's "it" in their games. I and a medic from 2nd Platoon were picked.

As the LT and I headed down the trench to our platoon area, he said he was glad I was going because the other medic was new to our outfit. I went on to our medical bunker to stock up my aid kits. Two things were in our favor. One, the weather—it was a nice spring day. Two, no moon—we'd be under cover in complete darkness. When you go sneaking into enemy territory, you need all the advantages you can get.

The mission was to be eight hours long. The code name was *Puzzle*, and the password to get out and back through the wire was *jig*, counter *saw*. Once we got into no man's land in the valley, the first eight troopers went into a diamond formation with the LT, the radioman and interpreter, and us medics in the middle. The other men got into a diamond formation behind us. No man's land was full of tall grasses and weeds. We were on the lookout for an ambush. The valley was wide, with steep hills on the left and right. The LT decided to take the high road, literally, to stay above the village. We would have a difficult journey up and down the rough sides of the hill, but the name of the game was surprise.

The sun was about to go down behind the mountains. The valley would be dark in about a half hour. As we moved along the hillside, we went single-file, staying ten feet apart. Heavy foliage made it doubly difficult to spot the enemy, but equally hard for them to see us. The advance now was a slow go over rough terrain. Several of the men stumbled. They were back on their feet quickly with bloody, dirt-covered hands. The LT had them fall back to where we medics were. On the move, we took care of their wounds.

Someone was coming our way. Our two scouts popped back into view to tell us four North Koreans were approaching with weapons over their shoulders. It looked like they were out for an evening hike, not looking for us. They would have to cross a small gully ahead to get to us. The LT decided we'd lie in wait on the ridge above the gully and when the North Koreans had entered it, our sharpshooters would pick them off, silencers on, all at the same time.

The LT and the sharpshooters, scopes on, took up their position just above the gully some fifty feet away. We waited in silence. Looking through his night field glasses, the LT saw the four soldiers—they had stopped in the gully to take a leak. He gave a hand signal to the sharpshooters. Their shots went off like clockwork with one sound. The enemy dropped in their tracks. Our troops took their weapons, then dragged the bodies to a grassy area and covered them with branches. We had about a half hour more to go before reaching our objective, the village. The night was black, but the stars gave a bit of light.

We moved to a shallow gully in the cliff, about two hundred yards above the village. From there we could see an old rice storage building where our buddies were being held. The report at base said the floor plan of the building was simple, like an army barracks. A long hallway went down the middle, with exit doors at each end and three small rooms on each side of the hallway. The two middle rooms held our guys. The windows had bars. The four end rooms housed two guards each. A dirt path some one hundred yards long led to the village itself. On each side of the building were two large rice paddies. Behind the building was open land.

We moved down the cliff to the rice paddy below and crept to within one hundred feet of the building. Dim light shone from the windows. The LT sent four men to scout the area and look in the windows. Two guards were in each of the end rooms, sitting on their beds with their weapons hanging on the wall. The prisoners' rooms had heavy bars on the windows. The intelligence report was right on the mark.

My buddy medic went with the first eight troops to take out the guards in the front two rooms. I went with the other eight troops who would take out the guards in the back two rooms and snatch and grab our prisoners. The LT, our radioman, and our interpreter stayed in the rice paddy to watch for trouble and cover our exit.

We took off, staying close to the building, working our way to the back. I was to stay back a ways from the building, in the open field, to take care of any injured. One minute and counting. Pistols loaded, silencers on. Ready.

Seconds ticked off. I was ready for the worst, and also ready to make like a bat out of hell once the prisoners came out. The men took off. As the back door opened, light streamed out from inside the building. *Pfft-pfft,* and seconds later our troops and six prisoners ran out of the building. "Let's go, Doc, head for the paddy!"

The rescue took just fifteen minutes. We made a silent, mad dash to meet up in the rice paddy, then off we scrambled back to the cliff. Before heading up the steep slope, I looked back through the darkness. The lights were still on in the building. The village was quiet. No one had seen or heard us.

We began a fast track for home base. I told the LT we had to stop somewhere soon to check the injuries of our rescued men. They were probably hungry and thirsty. If we didn't stop and tend to them, they might not be able to make the journey back. "Okay, Doc, you're the boss."

We went into a wooded area. The LT set up a guard perimeter around us medics. The former prisoners drank up the water from our canteens, saying it was their first water in two days. The troops had permission to dig into their rations, and we medics went around gathering enough food from them to feed our rescued guys. Tonight's menu, in the dark without candles, was cold beans and franks and fruit cocktail. I pulled my trusty church key—my can opener—out of my aid kit. The men wolfed down their food. I saved a candy bar each for the six men to have later. They sure deserved a treat.

While everyone ate, my buddy medic took care of a gash on one man's arm. I took care of a guy with a cut on his calf. I gave aspirins to the two with headaches. The LT asked about the mens' wounds and said we had to get out of the area fast. I said, "We'll watch after them. Let's give it a go!"

We took off again. Next stop would be home base. We zigzagged and climbed up and down through some of the most difficult terrain I've ever been in. If it was bad on us, how much worse it must be for the troopers we had rescued. I kept telling them to drink plenty of water and to hang in there.

There's that old saying, *we aren't out of the woods yet*. We had about two hours to go before reaching no man's land and then pay dirt—home. For the next hour or so, we slowly worked our way down to the valley below. Once there, we had five hundred yards more to get to their front line. We were thinking we had it made when our two scouts came running back. Fifteen North Korean soldiers were in the valley in an open area ahead, right where we planned to go through.

We had one big advantage—we knew where they were, but they had no idea we were nearby. Our two scouts and our interpreter went down the side of the hill. The darkness and thick foliage helped them get close enough to hear what the enemy were up to. They were sitting on logs, taking a break.

The LT told the freed prisoners and our radioman to get behind our formation and stay low. When he gave the signal, they were to run like hell through the enemy lines to no man's land and home. Our interpreter and us two docs were staying with the LT and his men to execute the plan. Surprise was paramount.

My buddy medic went with eight men to an area to our right. Each of our two groups would get into a semicircle and take out the enemy with silenced pistols. We were set at our end, hoping everything was okay with the others. One minute and counting. The gooks were loud, having a good time drinking. At the signal, our men fired. *Pfft-pfft*.

We all beat a fast track heading through enemy lines. We met up at our rendezvous area in no man's land. At 0200 hours, we gave the password and crossed over the wire to home base. I'll always remember those four words—*Eeny, Meeny Miny Moe*.

CHAPTER 11

BADASS BOYS

Forty men were told they would be gone "until the mission was complete." The unit was called the "Badass Boys." Most of the men were especially chosen from our battalion. These troopers were the toughest and meanest fighters we had. Guys who could stick a knife into a person's back and twist it and think nothing of it. We all had cover stories. Mine was that I would be gone for a few days to help the overworked staff in the burn unit at the battalion aid station.

Military Police took the men away to a secret rear echelon area where they'd spend two days going over explosives, compass reading, cliff climbing, hand-to-hand combat, and night warfare tactics, and they'd complete a brutal physical training program. We medics and litter-bearers would meet up with them later.

I was asked to oversee the other medics since I had several such missions already under my belt. I headed down our hill to a waiting litter jeep for the half-mile ride to the BAS. There I met up with a major who helped me get supplies. We often ran out of zinc oxide salve, which is a good ointment for battle wounds and burns, and hydrogen peroxide solution, which is a first-aid antiseptic. I filled the other four medics' aid kits. I packed gauze, tape, ammonia capsules, aspirins, safety pins, sulfa powder, alcohol pads, and methylate. We needed scalpels, scissors, compresses, hypodermic needles, syringes of morphine, and bismuth and paregoric for stomach and intestinal problems. I put in arm slings, thermometers, penlights, pens, matches, and quinine tablets. And don't forget the field EMTs for tagging the wounded and the dead. I filled an extra medical bag that I could carry over my shoulder, just in case.

Our objective was a village a few miles down the valley. It was in our sector so we were familiar with the area. Our leader was a full bird colonel we were to call Number 1. Each of five teams had a burp gun, taken from the enemy, which could shoot some 800 to 900 rounds per minute. They were Soviet PPSh submachine guns or the Chinese version, and made a rapid bup-bup-bup noise that gave them their nickname. Every member of the unit, including the medics, carried .45 caliber pistols with silencers. We strapped trench knives to our legs. We wore faded fatigues, black soft fatigue caps instead of helmets, black tennis shoes with black shoestrings, and black socks. Our faces and arms and the backs of our hands were blackened with special ointment. We wore flak jackets and each of us carried a two-day supply of C-rations. We would use clickers to communicate.

We medics made sure all dog tags were taped down and that the men had taped their pants at the ankles so the legs wouldn't catch on anything or ride up and expose their skin to scratches from weeds or bushes. It was a muggy 80-degree evening and everyone was to have two canteens full of water. I did not want any of the men to get dehydration or heat exhaustion.

Some of the men from our battalion hadn't been on a mission like this before. I asked one of the guys from my squad why he had agreed to go. "It sounds exciting. Plus, Doc, you're going!" he laughed.

Number 1 planned to utilize his well-armed unit to take out the ammo and fuel dumps, the radio shack, and a railroad bridge. "The mission is critical," he said. "Without it, our advance to the north will be much more difficult."

Our password was *Baseball*. The counter was *World Series*. In case a member of our unit got lost and needed to get back through our front line on his own, the special code name *Badass Boys* was to be used. Number 1 went on, "Remember—teamwork! And one last thing, we will not abandon anyone, dead or alive."

Back at our front line, we headed down through our minefields in the dark and made it to our rendezvous area below our hill. Number 1 radioed back to base, "This is the Badass Boys at home plate heading to first base, over and out."

We got into a diamond formation. Team 5 with Number 1, the interpreter, the radioman, and me, was in the middle. We made it through no man's land with Lady Luck on our side. We gathered around Number 1 to hide the light from his penlight while he looked at the map. "To our left, just below the enemy's hill, there's a dried up creek bed that runs all the way up to the village. We'll follow that."

The shallow creek bed gave us good cover, but it was full of debris from past battles. Rubbish and rubble of all kinds were scattered around the remains of jeeps and trucks. We made it about one hundred yards when we heard one click. Enemy soldiers were up on the hill. After they moved on, we silently inched our way further along. As we got past most of the debris, Number 1 whispered, "Now that we don't have all that shit in front of us, we should be at first base in thirty minutes."

The night was eerily still and quiet as a prayer. Usually we heard strange noises from insects and unknown animals that could help disguise the noise of our clickers. First base was in sight. Team 5, including me, and the leaders from the other teams went to check out the area. Faint lights shone from the village. Number 1 radioed back to home base. "This is the Badass Boys at first base." He listened for a few minutes. "Over and out." He told us home base wanted us to *steal a base*, which was code meaning a trainload of supplies was coming *this* morning at 0330 hours, not the next morning. We would not have to spend time waiting it out in a cave somewhere.

We hightailed it back to the rest of the unit and Number 1 told them the change of plans. As jump-off time neared, we got into a huddle. "Once we get to the railroad bridge, we'll split up for our targets. Our rendezvous area will be here and we'll leave at 0300 hours sharp. Everybody knows what to do. The Team 2 BAR man, our radioman, and all litter-bearers will stay here to cover our exit. When the train comes at 0330 hours and sets off the charges, we'll be long gone. Synchronize your watches."

I'd be lying if I didn't say I was a little nervous. I was with Team 1 and their medic. Our sharpshooter would take out the bridge guard. He scooted up to a low mound where he could get a clear shot. Wasting no time, he took aim and the guard slumped over. With our sharpshooter covering me, I crawled toward the body. A dim light from the bridge shone over it. I threw a small rock, hitting the body. No movement. I made my way to the bridge. Reaching the guard, I pulled his body up and leaned it back against the bridge frame. The bullet had hit dead center through the head.

Our sharpshooter and BAR man set up nearby as lookouts. Our demolitions team carefully attached explosives under both sides of the bridge. The delay fuses on our four targets would give us plenty of time to beat a fast track out before the explosives went off. Enemy troops were in a staging area waiting to make their way down the valley, and the train would have four cars loaded with supplies for them. The locomotive's front wheels rolling over the pressure switch would set things in motion. The bridge would explode with the train on it and trigger explosives at the other three target areas. The enemy would think we were still in the area and look for us around the village, when in fact we would be half an hour away by then. The noise of the explosions would be like having a thousand fireworks going off at the same time. What a surprise waited for the enemy.

I was sent to check on our guards. When I returned, our demo guys were taping the last explosives to the last support beam. Then we heard the special five clicks. Someone was coming. We cocked our weapons and froze. Soon we heard one click. Our leader gave one click back. He whispered, "Could be a trap. A gook could be pretending he's one of us." He motioned me to follow him topside. Up on the bridge he gave one click and received one in response. He whispered, "On what team did Babe Ruth and Lou Gehrig play?"

"New York Yankees."

We made our way toward a body lying face down ahead of us. It was a North Korean soldier. In the dim light, I saw he had gone by way of the knife—a big wound to the back. I felt for a heartbeat and found none. We now had two dead enemy soldiers. Our leader and sharpshooter carried them away from the bridge area and covered them with brush.

We left, leapfrogging to our rendezvous area with our BAR man behind covering our backside. As we approached, our leader stopped…*Click. Click* came a response. "*Baseball*," came a whisper. "*World Series*," our leader answered. Our lookout team had all weapons drawn. We were the first to arrive. Then came Teams 2 and 3. A litter-bearer kept count as the men checked in. With two minutes left, up jumped Number 1 and Team 4. All here! We headed back to second base—the creek bed. When we reached it, Number 1 said, "We have to make faster time." We took off again, our pace picked up so we would be a good distance away when the blast went off. The debris in the creek bed was a bitch, but in a way good for us. We could hide around it if we had to. On the other hand, if we made any noise going through, the enemy would be on us like dogs chasing cats.

We got back into diamond formation. A BAR man and a sharpshooter took the point. At 0325 we stopped and turned to watch the fireworks. The whole village erupted in a giant column of smoke and flames. Even from where we were, it was a huge display. There was no time to celebrate because we had to get out of there fast, but the teams knew they had done their job well and Number 1 gave us two thumbs up.

Number 1 radioed to home base, "This is the Badass Boys at second base heading to third, over and out." He whispered, "Let's get our asses out of here." With two clicks we started out again. We had to keep a look out for trip wires and booby traps. We had evaded the enemy so far, but for how long?

We neared the edge of no man's land. Waiting for us were our two point men. A small patrol of eight enemy had just passed above us on the hill, going in the direction of the village. Number 1 whispered, "Maybe the hunt is on for us, so let's be ready." Teams 1 and 2 made their way into no man's land. Just as their last two men were across, the shit hit the fan.

"Code Red! Ambush!" The firing came from high on the hill above us. My Team 5 was caught between the creek bed and no man's land, pinned down by a shower of bullets and grenades. "Help! Team 2!" I told our interpreter to stay put and cover Teams 3 and 4 when they crossed the enemy line. The radioman would cover me with his burp gun. I was the closest medic to the cries and I was going for them. I yelled for two litter-bearers, took a deep breath, and off I went, my heart beating loud and fast. Bullets ricocheted all around as I crawled forward on all fours toward the wounded. The noise of the BARs and the burp guns and of grenades exploding was deafening. Without hesitation, our radioman deliberately exposed himself to enemy fire to draw attention away from me and our two wounded. His act gained me enough time to move the wounded out of the line of fire. I could tell from cries behind me that the medics of Teams 1 and 2 had their hands full.

Both wounded were in a lot of pain. A grenade blast had sprayed shrapnel over one man. I took care of him first, then went to work on the other guy. He had twisted his ankle from a fall. I felt for broken bones, but it seemed like just a bad sprain. I took off his tennis shoe and sock, grabbed an Ace bandage from my shoulder aid bag, and wrapped his ankle to keep the swelling down. On went the sock and shoe, then I taped around his shoe and ankle for more support until we got back to home base. The litter guys transported them into no man's land. During this time our radioman had been moving between alternate positions of cover, engaging the gooks with some of their own medicine—the burp gun.

Number 1 yelled, "Teams 1 and 2, start firing! Demo men, use your leftover explosives on the hill!" Teams 1 and 2 blasted the hell out of the top of the hill. "Blast 'til the last son of a bitch is dead!"

Teams 3 and 4 ran for no man's land, one of them yelling, "The hill's going up!" Dirt and rocks went flying. If any enemy back at the village didn't know our whereabouts before, they sure did now.

We moved quietly through the thick bushes and high grass, keeping the wounded and the litter-bearers in mind. At one click we dropped to the ground. Our point men had heard talking ahead. Number 1 and our Korean interpreter crawled closer. Eight North Korean soldiers were standing around taking a smoking break. They were out looking for us. Number 1 signaled Team 3 and our two point men to take out the soldiers. He whispered, "Doc, tag along to make sure all the gooks are dead."

We were back soon. All eight were for sure dead. We had gone another hundred yards when we again heard one click. Again we hugged the ground. A loud noise was approaching off to the right. Number 1 whispered, "Hold your fire until I give the word." Four deer went running across our path. We took a break for water and we medics checked on our wounded. The men were damn glad the mission was almost over. We were filthy and stunk like hogs. It was a miracle we had all made it through alive.

Number 1 got on the radio to home base. "We're rounding third and about to score a home run." But home base had altered the plans. We were to go to a new reading. We took off with Number 1 in the lead again. The sky had lightened. With one click from Number 1 we stopped in our tracks. He seemed to be waiting for something. *Click*—"Who goes?"

"Badass Boys . . . *Baseball*."

"*World Series.*"

We rounded an area of brush and there waiting for us was the same major who had helped me get medical supplies. Standing next to him was a full bird colonel medical officer. Behind them waiting to take us all back to the rear echelon were four military trucks, an MP jeep in the lead and one in the rear. Litter jeeps were ready for our wounded. In front of them were two more MP jeeps, with a one-star general standing beside each. What a nice welcome party!

I asked the Major, "Sir, would you put in the mission report that Doc said 'Brilliant successes were in large measure a result of the determined spirit of the whole unit and of the sound leadership of Number 1.'" He laughed and said he would.

The Major said, "I'd like to say a few words on behalf of home base and the front line troops. "What you did made it easier for our advancing troops. You did your job well. Thank you."

Number 1 said, "Men, I'm damned pleased and proud of all of you. I can see why they called this unit the Badass Boys." I told him, "If I ever have to go on another mission like this, you're the kind of man I'd want to lead it."

"Thanks, Doc, you're okay." As his jeep drove off, Number 1 turned and gave us two thumbs up. I, too, could see why they called this team the Badass Boys.

CHAPTER 12

DAWN OF ANOTHER DAY

Three medics had died, all killed in action. We learned the hard way about the nature of our enemy. In Korea, the enemy snipers would deliberately aim to kill the medics. They probably believed this would destroy the morale of the soldiers, to know they would have no first-aid care in the field. They blatantly ignored the fourth Geneva Convention agreement many nations had signed in 1949. It reaffirmed that medical troops would be considered unarmed non-combatants. The Red Cross International was recognized as a neutral group. Medical personnel would wear red crosses on their arms and helmets to show their jobs were not to kill, but to save lives. Each side was to respect the other's doctors, medics, and corpsmen.

At first I did wear the Red Cross arm bands as well as the Red Cross emblem on my helmet. However, once experience demonstrated that the enemy acutely singled out those red crosses, I felt I would stay alive longer if I did not wear them. Those big emblems were a good bulls-eye target to shoot at. Most combat medics now simply wore their fatigues without any special markings. We were recognized on the battlefield by our unique equipment, the most prominent being the aid kits strapped across our backsides, banging against our butts as we ran. Medics who didn't used to carry a weapon were doing so now. I carried a dagger on the belt of my aid kit for my own protection, but I also wore a shoulder holster carrying a .45-caliber pistol, the standard Army sidearm.

I had been in Korea now for about six months, and this was my first day with this new company. My platoon leader, a lieutenant, was an okay guy. He said, "I'm glad to have a medic with your experience. I hear you've been in a lot of battles." The company was a replacement, and this was their first full month on line. The LT's platoon had only one medic left, and now I would make two. We would each have to cover twenty-six men, and maybe more depending on how the fighting went. That was too many. I was glad to see the trench was dug shoulder deep across the front slopes, so as I went from one end to the other I'd only have to duck my head to stay hidden. In the company I had come from, the trenches were dug only chest high, if that.

Being on our front lines, going on patrols, raids, and missions, I realized how good my training had been at the Army medical schools. I had taken classes in anatomy and physiology, on minor surgery and first aid (MSFA), and on temperature-pressure-respiration (TPR). I had a class called Operating Room (OR). I learned about all types of shots, and about broken bones, fractures, blood transfusions, and poisonous gases. Then again, you can read all the books you want and go to all the classes, but once the first bullet flies over your head, all bets are off. The name of the game is saving lives using whatever means it takes. I kept some of my medical books with me and from time to time I went over them. There was always something more to learn and improve on.

The weather was super. The sun was just going down and the temperature was 85 degrees. Things were quiet with only a few rounds landing here and there below our hill. I was sitting on my wire bunk shooting the bull with some of the other medics when we got a call from our platoon leader. There was some rumble far up the valley. All units up!

We were on full red alert. Soon we heard the familiar sounds of bugles, whistles and horns, and the banging of sticks. Yelling, screaming Chinese came across the valley floor. The incoming mail of enemy artillery and mortar rounds hit us. This is where I earn my keep! We medics and litter-bearers took up our positions and waited. This time the enemy had another weapon. They quieted down and called out over a loudspeaker, "Charlie, give up. Bobby, give up." They called out some other names in English, I guess hoping they would get to one of the troopers' names and make him think they knew him personally. They were playing mind games. In the past, I'd heard them shouting things like, "Do you miss your wife and those home-cooked meals?" Anything to try to shake us up. And they'd say it in good English, too, in male and female voices. I think all those messages were tape-recorded, because one time we found some of the tapes.

Under the moonlight, we saw the enemy coming in waves, one after another, about a hundred yards apart. More incoming mail, this time only mortar rounds. Our outgoing mail flew over our heads, landing in the valley below and killing hundreds. The rest of the enemy swarmed up our hill like a herd of stampeding cattle. As our flares went up we saw rolls upon rolls of them, as far as we could see. The enemy came pouring up and through our minefields, acting like the mines were not even there. Our BAR men and machine gunners mowed them down, bodies stacking like cordwood. Then we were overrun and the men were in hand-to-hand combat. They used gun butts, bayonets, and knives. It was all for one and one for all.

Our troops had been fighting now for an hour and a half. We medics were patching up our wounded as fast as we could. The litter-bearers were busy as hell. A soldier came running up to me. I was just finishing a tape job on a wounded leg. "Doc, Doc, would you look at my buddy?" With bullets zipping over our heads, we ran to Area 2. When we got to the wounded, I found a piece of shrapnel had lacerated his pulmonary artery. I fought frantically to save him, but to no avail. He died in his buddy's arms. I tagged him KIA. "Doc, please Doc, Area 1!" Making my way back, I had to step over five or six dead Chinese. Our wounded man had been stabbed with a bayonet. "Can you help me, Doc?"

"Lie still and hang in there. You'll be okay and in the arms of a pretty girl soon." The soldier was holding his left side, bleeding badly, and in a lot of pain. I stopped the bleeding the best I could and cleaned the wound. I bandaged him up and gave him a shot of morphine. Two of his buddies ran over. "Doc, he saved us! He did it alone!" I said, "I'll put him in for a Silver Star along with his Purple Heart." They took off, yelling their thanks. On the back of the EMT I wrote my brief recommendations for the medals. The Silver Star is one type of medal for bravery in combat, and the Purple Heart is given for soldiers killed in combat or wounded—I only marked that for men with more serious wounds, not just being grazed a little by a bullet. No telling if the soldier would get the medals as that was decided by higher ups.

"Doc!" came from Area 3. As I got there a mortar landed some twenty yards forward of the trench line. Shrapnel flew in every direction. The blast threw me backward and I lay dazed. Shaking the cobwebs clear, my ears still ringing, I crawled down the trench toward the cry for help, mortars coming in all around. The trooper was not wearing his flak jacket and had been hit bad. Probably by a mortar round by the way his body was torn—ragged flesh everywhere. His chest was open and bloody, and I knew it was just a matter of time. His eyes said everything. I dragged him into the bunker behind us and held him in my arms. My sleeves were soaked red with his blood. I told him he'd fought a good fight. His voice was a whisper, "Doc, I hope I didn't let the troops down." I told him he had saved us all. He slumped over. At least he didn't die alone.

Near midnight, we were still taking a lot of casualties. I ran across a soldier lying in the trench. As I leaned in to patch him up, he said, "Doc, we got company." A Chinese had jumped down some twenty feet away. I stood up. We were face to face. He had a knife in his right hand. My gun was in its holster, strapped to my left shoulder. I thought of what a commando had told me once. I said I had never fired a weapon at a man before. "It's easy, Doc. Just point and pull the trigger."

I pulled out the .45, pointed it with one hand, and pulled the trigger. The recoil kicked back hard into my shoulder. The Chink dropped dead two feet in front of us. "Thanks, Doc, you're one helluva shot," our wounded trooper told me. I patched him up and headed back to Area 1.

"Doc!" Mortars landed all over the place as I crawled on all fours, bullets flying up and down the trenches. I found two of our troopers hit. One had taken a bullet to the arm. The other had been hit in the head and was unconscious. The wound was bad. Real bad. I went to work on him, but he died within minutes. I turned to the other soldier, ripped open his shirt, and told him he was one lucky guy. The bullet had only grazed him. I cleaned the wound, bandaged him, and tagged him WIA. "You're okay to fight," I told him, and off he went down the trench.

Our front line troops were having a bitch of a time. It seemed the whole damn Chinese army was out there. Mortars were flying in again like they were celebrating New Year's Eve. I hugged the dirt walls of our trenches as rounds of mortars slammed in, shrapnel blasting through the air. Anyone out and about was surely dead or badly wounded. We had a saying about the Chinese and their mortars—*you could throw a dime out of your bunker and they would hit it and give you change*. They were that good.

The shelling stopped. Dirt covered me from head to toe. I shook myself off and crawled towards the sound of agonized cries. Above the trench lines, I could hear the fire of automatic weapons. Crawling over dead Chinese bodies, I found a scene of devastation. The trench line was no more, just a big pile of dirt. With the help of our litter-bearers, we managed to pull out the most seriously wounded man. I decided to give him a unit of plasma. The litter-bearers carried him into one of the bunkers on the back slopes. One of the litter-bearers held up my penlight. Once I had the plasma started, I let the litter-bearers finish up. I headed back to our forward slope with bullets zipping overhead and went to work on three soldiers full of shrapnel. If it weren't for their flak jackets, it could have been much worse.

It was impossible for us medics to make our way up and down

our trenches without crawling around a dead or dismembered body. Our machine gunners kept spraying the onrushing Chinese, but no sooner did one drop, then another took his place. They swarmed up our hill like bees, overwhelming us by their numbers. We were so low on litters that some of our troops helped put the wounded on their own ponchos and field jackets and carried them to the aid station down our back slope. The stench of death was everywhere. I asked one of the litter-bearers to get me more battle dressings and morphine next time he ran by the aid station.

I ran across one of our troopers lying still in the trench. A large piece of shrapnel had pierced his helmet and lodged in his neck. I listened to his chest and felt for his carotid artery, but he was dead. The litter-bearers following me would tag him KIA. I continued on my way to Area 2. Halfway there, a barrage of mortars hit fifteen to twenty yards in front of me. The explosion cracked the air. I flew up and fell back down. My ears were ringing like hell from the blast wave, but I jumped up, none the worse, and began crawling over piles of trench line dirt caved in from the shelling.

"Doc, Doc, help!" When the litter-bearers arrived they helped uncover the men buried in rubble. Of the seven we found, three were wounded and four were dead. The wounded had shrapnel embedded everywhere. After I tended to the worst of them, our litter-bearers took them off down to our aid station for more treatment. No sooner had they left, than an endless stream of our artillery and mortar rounds flooded the valley below. Gunfire cackled as bullets whizzed overhead.

The battle raged for two and a half more hours. There was little doubt that we had inflicted tremendous damage on the enemy. At dawn, what was left of them ran down into the valley and faded into the hills across no man's land. The Chinese very seldom attacked during the day. After a night of hell, we were still alive and damn tired of getting our asses kicked. Looking over our hill covered with dead Chinese bodies, I noticed many of them didn't have weapons and were barefoot.

Now came the hard part, the mop up—looking for more of our wounded and counting our losses. Afterwards, I asked the Captain if we could clean out our sector. Corpses and body parts filled our trenches, and the air reeked with the stench of blood and death. We medics were concerned that in the hot weather this might spread disease among our troops. "You're in charge," he said.

For the next two and a half days, our engineers went about rebuilding our broken-down trench lines and bulldozing the thousands of dead Chinese into mass graves. Those of us who were lucky enough to have survived will never forget that night. It was hell. War is a bitch. I didn't think I would live to see the dawn of another day.

CHAPTER 13

CODE NAME L-7

I was going on a mission, code name *L-7*. The L was for *Lightning*, getting in and out fast. The 7 was for the six commandos and me. We had four explosives and munitions experts—two Brits and two Aussies. The radioman and interpreter were ROK. All of us trained for four days. The explosives experts practiced blowing things up and doing whatever else commandos do. The radioman worked on the coded messages. The interpreter brushed up on the four languages he could read, write, and speak—Korean, Chinese, Japanese, and English. I memorized the medical make-up of each man on the team. We developed a bond in the short time we had together. The men had to know they could count on each other and on me to take care of them when things got hot and heavy.

We were each called by numbers. The explosives men were numbered 1 to 4. The radioman was Number 5, the interpreter was Number 6, and I was Number 7. No one knew the others' real names and for good reason. If anything went awry we could disavow everything. If we were captured, we didn't know anything about the others' names or ranks. The mission happened, but it didn't happen.

We would use codes for transmitting and receiving messages to and from home base, and also for transmitting our positions and my medical reports. Our destination was *sunrise*, and *sunset* meant home base. *Sundown* meant we were moving out. For medical reports, *shining moon* meant all were okay, *full moon* meant dead, *half moon* meant wounded. Our objectives were coded simply, like PP for power plant and RD for railroad depot.

These guys were tough, the kind who sought out and welcomed conflict and risk. They were handpicked for their expertise and were aggressive, independent, and not modest about their competence. I felt okay with them because they radiated authority, courage, and responsibility. They were the best of the best. My job was to get all six commandos and myself back alive, and I was up for it.

The night before the mission, I filled my aid kits and a surgical backpack for a two-day trip. I loaded up on battle dressings, bandages, gauze pads, slings, and tourniquets. I put in antibiotic ointment packs, alcohol cleaning pads, mentholated analgesic cream, morphine, penicillin, cascara sagrata laxative, paregoric for diarrhea, and quinine pills for malaria. I added mosquito repellent, salt tablets, and water purification tablets. I also put in, and kept that to myself, fourteen cyanide capsules in case something went really wrong. Then I could give each man two capsules to put under his tongue, and in a minute or so, good-bye us. On top of all this, I carried two days' worth of C-rations.

As I was packing, so were the other men. They had everything needed to hold off an army: all kinds of plastic explosives, TNT, daggers, knives, grenades, BARs, burp guns, and flares. We were issued the latest weapons and wore the bulletproof vests with armor plates in them. The vests were stiff, cumbersome, and heavy, but I was damn glad to have one since I was often out in the open when tending our wounded. Like everyone else in our group, I had a .45 caliber pistol in a shoulder holster strapped to my left side.

Our take-off time was 2000 hours (8:00 p.m.). Commando Number 4 was our leader, not just because of his fighting abilities, but because of his technical and logistical skills as well. Our mission was to conduct raids on enemy power plants, ammo depots, bridges, and railroad depots. I taped together each man's dog tags to keep them from rattling.

We passed through our MLR and headed single file, ten feet apart, down our hill through the 1,500 winding yards of our minefield. I was near the end, with Numbers 3 and 4 in the rear. We held onto the guide wire with the white flags attached—the safe color for the day. We could touch nothing else, not a tree or bush along the way, because it might be rigged with tripwires for certain death.

After forty-five minutes we made it to the valley below and through no man's land to the enemy front line. The night was cloudy. Number 4 was surprised we had met no resistance since our intelligence reports had it there was a rag-tag Chinese unit in this sector. We took a break to go over our next move while Numbers 1 and 2 left to scout out the area. They found two guards sitting around a small fire. We'd have to take them out. Number 4 said, "Do it." The scouts left to take care of things.

We crossed the enemy front line and headed north to our first destination, a small town about an hour or so away. Ten minutes down the path, we took cover along a stream as a five-man patrol went by. We reached the village by midnight, stopping two hundred yards away in a large rice paddy for a sip of water from our canteens and some last minute details. The radioman and interpreter sent a message to home base. In Japanese, the interpreter said we had made *sunrise* and all was *shining moon.*

Numbers 1 and 2 took off upstream to scout the bridge that led to the village. We had an hour to pull off the raid on the bridge, the railroad depot, and the large power plant. Our radioman set up his BAR in the rice paddy to cover our exit. I was to stay with him. The other commandos would set charges to go off ten minutes apart as we all hightailed it out. I wished them all good luck.

On the dot, our commandos came running back and just as they jumped into the rice paddy, the shit hit the fan. The power plant went first, blowing sky high and leaving the town with no lights. Number 4 said, "Let's get the hell out of here—fast!" We backtracked through the paddy, heading into a wooded area about a hundred yards away. As we got there, the railroad depot went off. The sky filled with smoke and fire. We had hoped to be farther away, so we ran double-time. I ran with everything in me, trying to keep up. Every time I took a step, my two aid kits smacked me in the butt. I was not about to say anything, but I was pooped! In the distance we heard the final blast destroying the bridge.

Number 4 decided we had gone far enough. We found a small cave in the side of a hill and took cover there. I took care of one man's wrist injury and a cut on another man's thumb. A tarp was hung over the cave entrance so my penlight wouldn't be noticed by the enemy. While I worked on the men, I asked how the raid had gone. Number 4 said all went as planned except they had to take out three enemy, strangling them with commo wire.

By 0300 hours, we were ready for some shut-eye, with the men taking turns guarding the entrance. We would have a long rest since we weren't leaving until late afternoon. We woke to eat our C-rations as Number 5 radioed to home base and said we were *sunup*, ready for the next *sunrise*. We were *shining moon*, and *PP, RD* and *RDP* had all gone well. Then Number 4 went over details for our next raid, on an ammo depot not too far away. Intelligence said the depot had gotten a shipment two days ago and wouldn't get another for two weeks. Twelve Chinese were living in two huts and had a guard shelter. Number 4 said, "When we're done I'll be able to rub what's left out with my boot and leave no trace for the other Chinks to see."

We headed for an area of trees to use as cover. The terrain was such a bitch we took an extra half hour to get to our target destination. We were well-hidden in a wooded area about two hundred yards from the ammo depot. The valley was in deep shadows now with the sun behind the high mountains. Number 4 moved to the edge of the tree line and took out his high-powered night field glasses for a better look at the layout of the area, to make sure our intelligence reports were correct. We didn't want any slip-ups. Number 5 got on the radio and our interpreter gave a report in Japanese. Number 4 looked at me. "Get your pistol ready, we may need you."

Number 5 would hide the radio in the bushes at the edge of the tree line. The explosives experts would crawl up to the barbed wire fencing surrounding the depot. The rest of us would move to the only gate to the complex, with me carrying medical supplies and the others carrying TNT and bags of hand grenades. At the sound of the clicker, the explosives men would cut the wire and move to the inside, and at three clicks they would attack. The radioman and the interpreter carried burp guns and five clips of ammo each along with their pistols, in case any enemy made a mad dash to escape.

The moment of truth was here. The guards were talking pretty loud in their shelter. They seemed to be bored. Our men were now through the barbed wire. At three clicks, all hell broke loose. The commandos jumped up, blasting away with their guns and throwing grenades into the shelter. All four guards were killed instantly. Hearing the gunfire and explosions, six Chinese ran out of the huts, wearing just their shorts. When they saw us attacking, bullets flying, they turned back, but Number 4 opened up with his burp gun, killing three in a spray of fire. The others made it back into the huts.

Two enemy machine gunners at a nearby bunker opened up, shooting at anything that moved. We were pinned down. Number 1 crawled out of the guard shelter to within fifty yards of the bunker, then was hit by a bullet. "Number 7!" I crawled over and helped him back to the shelter under a rain of fire. He'd been hit in the upper arm. I stopped the bleeding with a tourniquet and cleaned and bandaged the wound the best I could in the dark. Lucky for us, no broken bones. I put his arm in a sling and told him to stay put, pistol ready.

Number 4 threw up a white flare to see exactly where the machine gunners were, yelling at Numbers 5 and 6 to get their grenades ready. Then a red flare went up and grenades blasted left and right, landing all over the bunker area. The machine guns went quiet. Another white flare shot up. Both gunners lay over their weapons, dead.

Two big blasts came from the direction of the huts. Number 3 had hit them with TNT and smoke was pouring out. The enemy lay dead. We counted quickly—ten, eleven, twelve! Now we had to blow up the ammo before the whole Chinese army arrived. I stayed on a low mound out of the way, acting as lookout and watching the commandos set charges. Within an hour they were done, charges set to go off in thirty minutes.

We headed back to the woods where we stopped a minute so I could tag Number 1 with what I had done for treatment and quickly take care of some of the other men with lesser wounds. We all took a couple sips of water, then left for home base. From a distance, we heard the ammo depot explode. After five hours, we crossed over our MLR. It was nearly dawn.

Waiting for us was a full bird colonel and six jeeps that took us a few miles to a big tent guarded by military police. Inside were five high-ranking officers. We sat at a long table full of snacks and drinks. After two hours of debriefing, we were done—dead tired, dirty, and glad it was all over. Number 4 came over to me. "Number 7, from all the men on the L-7 team, thank you for going. You're the best."

I shook hands with each of the commandos. "It was an honor to go with the best of the best."

contd. - Lynx Red Heros

Aid man, P.F.C. William J. Anderson, did an outstanding job of administering aid to the wounded men in the midst of the battle.

After being surprised and surrounded by the Chinese platoon, the men made it back to the line with only four wounded, and three of the wounded men received commendations for outstanding heroism. The tally of eight Chinese killed made the men feel rather good after it was all over.

AN "A.P. REPORTER YES, THATS A "STAR" ON THE "JEEP" TAKING ME DOWN THIS HILL!

CHAPTER 14

QUIET FOR A MOMENT

Sometimes things were quiet on the front line, but we were always on guard because the enemy would launch mortars at us every now and then to let us know they were alive and well. Of course, we would launch mortars back at them. The troops cleaned their weapons, restocked supplies and ammo, and generally got ready for the next battle, which could come at any time. If they had any spare time, they'd shoot craps, read their mail, or shoot the bull. We medics kept busy with our rounds, paperwork, checking on injuries from the last battle, and restocking medical supplies. We spent a lot of time picking bits of shrapnel out of the troops.

It was my job to keep the men battle ready, medically. I say they were men, but a lot of them were only seventeen or eighteen years old. Just boys. I had some guidelines I explained to the troops. They knew I'd be honest with them—that was a must. The name of the game was to keep them on the front line and in the trenches. My four simple rules were: one, if a fever didn't reach over 101, it wasn't high enough; two, if a wound didn't incapacitate them, it wasn't serious enough; three, if a trooper had a pain of some sort, I'd give him two aspirins; and four, if he had diarrhea, I'd give him the old reliable—paregoric.

As a medic, I had to cover all the bases. A common problem was self-inflicted shaving wounds—when we had time to shave. Water was at a premium. In the winter, the troops would melt snow in their canteen cups using the Coleman stoves in their heated bunkers. Yes, they would also use leftover coffee if necessary, reheated if possible. You do what you have to do. During cold weather, I told them to shave only once every three days. Myself, I had peach fuzz, so I'd shave every four days, if that. Mostly we never washed or took a shower or changed clothes. There wasn't water for that unless we were near a river or stream. We just made do with a cold "whore's bath," which meant a sponge bath. I carried medical grade green soap with me so if we were near a stream I could wade in and scrub the dried blood off my clothes.

The one thing we medics were not was dentists. We had troops ask us for toothbrushes, toothpaste, and dental floss. Remember, there was no water to waste. Most of our troops were in their late teens and early twenties, so many still had their wisdom teeth and had molar problems. We had nothing to ease their discomfort but aspirin. We did not have ice packs. We did not even have oil of clove, a common topical anesthesia.

Besides the ROK, we had some United Nations ally units—Aussie, Brit, and Turkish troops—strung out to the left and right of our 25th Infantry Division. We medics would go over sometimes to take care of the Turks, lining them up for shots or fixing them up if their medics needed help. They were fierce, tough-looking men, most with black beards or goatees and long mustaches turned up at the ends. They had long knives like machetes along with other weapons, and they brought back enemy trophies I won't say any more about. They didn't understand our language and we didn't understand theirs. We didn't spend too much time with them.

Every once in a while, our troops each got a carton of cigarettes and a case of Ballantine beer—that stuff tasted terrible to me, but it was a popular brand. I wasn't much of a drinker and I wasn't a smoker either. The guys would say, "Hey, Doc, you got a weed?" I sold some packs of cigarettes for a dollar each until some guys pulled me aside and told me I could sell one cigarette for a dollar. That's twenty dollars for the whole pack! I signed some kind of waiver so my share of any beer and cigarettes would be sold and the money put into my account. I got a lot of money from that.

Once I went to a USO show and saw the famous comedian Bob Hope and the actress Patricia Neal. The United Service Organization brought in entertainers to give the troops some fun and boost morale. Front line troops didn't often get to see the shows, but I had a minor wound one time when a six-inch piece of shrapnel dug a hole in my boot, and protocol was for me to stay off the front line for twenty-four hours. At the BAS I was given a ride to a nearby USO show. I met a trooper there from East St. Louis, Illinois, across the river from my state of Missouri. Kind of like finding a neighbor. During a break in the show we went on stage dressed in women's clothes and danced and lip-synced to the goofy "Rag Mop" song made popular by the Ames Brothers. The troops, sitting on the sloping ground around the stage, whooped it up and threw fruit they'd been given as snacks and empty drink cans at us—the stage had to be swept up before the next act could go on. Well, we weren't pretty like the USO show girls. Patricia Neal gave me a hug, though.

I learned enough Korean to speak "pig Latin" and understand a little. I learned from our ROK interpreters and the Korean houseboys we hired. These houseboys were young, often fourteen to fifteen years old, and many were probably orphans, their families killed in the war. They would show up out of nowhere. Our military screened them to try to get the ones that weren't trying to spy on us and give our position away.

When houseboys came to us they usually could not speak a word of English. We would use "sign language" to communicate. When we had time, we taught the boys English and they in turn taught us some Korean. During lulls in battle, houseboys worked from dawn to dusk. They kept things tidy, washed our clothes if we were near any creeks or rivers, and ran errands. They did whatever we asked, never once bitching about anything. One thing they did not do was clean our weapons.

For a while I had a houseboy who kept our medical bunker as clean as he could considering all the dirt around. Yes, dirt floors were the order of the day. Bunkers were either dug into the ground or built into the side of a hill along a fixed front line position. Sand bags were stacked eight to twelve feet high across the front of our aid bunkers in case a mortar round dropped in to say hello. Our medical aid bunkers were much larger than the bunkers of the front line troopers and were usually set on the back slope of a hill, safer from enemy fire. We made shelves, chairs, and tables out of old ammo crates. Besides our sleeping beds made of commo wire, we had two army cots to lay the wounded on so we could pull shrapnel out of them. This was for our walking wounded. We had medical lockers to store supplies in.

Our houseboy slept in the bunker with us. I'd give my kid chocolate from my C-rations. After a while he could speak pretty good English. We taught him to write English as well. He was far better at English than I was at Korean. I learned enough Korean to get along. That paid off big for me as a combat medic since I had to patch up South Korean good guys as well as any enemy North Korean or Chinese soldiers we took prisoner. The Chinese usually knew some Korean. Most of our interpreters could speak several languages, some up to six. Even some of our commandos could speak a few languages.

This houseboy I had was a good kid, really smart, and he could be trusted. I think his name was Kim Su-Won. He wanted to be a doctor so I took him under my wing. Sick calls on the front line are different from those done at the battalion aid stations farther back, where four to six medics and a couple doctors worked. The BAS had all our supplies, including whole blood and plasma flown in from our home front USA through Japan to Korea. Whole blood was kept in portable refrigerators run by generators. The BAS also had bottles of glucose and vials of penicillin, morphine, and tetanus vaccine. Jeeps brought in supplies from the BAS to our aid station and we combat medics did about everything except perform operations. Our houseboy learned a lot, and he survived—many did not. We medics, litter-bearers, and doctors collected enough money for him to go to a medical school in the States. I don't remember which one he went to.

Many of the soldiers and medics had pin-up girl calendars in their bunkers. After they came back from a patrol, they'd mark an X on the calendar date. That was a way to celebrate that they came back alive. One night, some of us medics were in our aid bunker arguing about who was the most beautiful woman of all. We decided on Elizabeth Taylor. She won our title of "Miss Aid Station." I wrote to Miss Taylor about this honor. She wrote back to thank us and enclosed an autographed picture of herself.

CHAPTER 15

SLIPPING AND SLIDDING

The smell of rain was in the air. I mean monsoon rain. Pouring rain day in and day out. When you have that much rain, you have mud—lots of mud.

This was our second day of pulling raids on villages and small towns on our trip north. Our next objective was a super big ammo dump a few miles ahead. Intelligence reports and aerial sightings suggested we might run into some 150 to 200 Chinese troops. They'd probably be poorly trained and badly equipped liked others we encountered, and hungry and war weary. It was our company's turn to take the lead. Our raiding party consisted of sixty-five troops, plus eight medics and twelve litter-bearers. The enemy would be hiding in every water hole, ditch, cave, trench, or gully they could find. We would hunt them down like rats. The constant downpours would make the terrain more difficult than it already was. Rice paddies looked like small lakes, and in some cases, small rivers.

We were in water from the get-go, up to a foot deep at times, slipping and falling our way to our objective. The night temperature was 93 degrees along with suffocating humidity. Rain came down in buckets. We climbed hills and slid down the other side. We waded in the mucky mud up to our calves. Our advance slowed to a crawl, but so far, so good. As we got closer, our company commander, the Captain, asked our platoon leader, the Lieutenant, to pick an advance scouting party from our platoon. Our platoon's sergeant led the party consisting of three BAR guys, three burp gunners, three sharpshooters, one radioman, and me. We were to stay in single file, ten feet apart, and travel five hundred yards ahead of our company.

The sky was getting light, but it was still raining cats and dogs when we came upon a wide valley. A village was about fifty yards ahead of us, with a large rice paddy to the right of it. A small hill overlooked the paddy and the village. We crept to the village and just as our point man entered it, the valley and village lit up like a Hollywood stage set. The enemy raked our scouting party with everything they had—machine guns, small arms, mortar fire. Our BAR point man was killed instantly. The rest of us took cover in a nearby small gully filled ankle deep with water and mud. Bullets flew over our heads and mortars blasted all around.

Sarge radioed back to the LT, "We got one man dead and eleven pinned down in a small gully just outside the village. Weapons fire coming from the small hill just above the rice paddy, to our right." The LT said he would get us all out before daybreak. He had a plan.

The gully was filling up fast with rain water. Ten minutes went by. Mortars were still coming in. One round exploded almost on top of us, scaring the living shit out of us. Then our battalion arrived firing rounds at the hill from big mortars set up on flatbed trucks. Ten of our battalion sharpshooters also came to the rescue. We made it out of the gully and back to the relative safety of our company.

As dawn came, our battalion commander, a colonel, held a staff meeting with all four company commanders and reminded them of our objective, the huge ammo dump in the village. We had to take the small hill to get beyond it. Companies 1 and 2 would take on the village, and Company 3 with our Company 4 would take on the hill. All would start at 0600 hours with a period of manmade thunder and lightning from our big mortars. No sooner said than done. The storm from our mortars lasted ten minutes. Chinese came running out of their caves and holes making all sorts of noises with tin cans, bugles, horns, and yelling.

The heavy rains made going up the hill exceptionally rough. Our troops slid, fell, picked themselves up, and kept going. The battle was far from over. Weapons fire flashed from the caves, holes and bunkers. It took four litter-bearers on each of the three stretchers to manhandle the wounded back down the rough, muddy terrain of the hill, an agonizing trip for all. I slogged through the mud, carrying some of the rifles of our wounded plus an aid kit full of dog tags that I'd taken off of our dead soldiers.

I had just rejoined the main body of our company midway up the hill, when I heard cries off to my left. Slipping and falling in the mud, I headed toward the sound. Bullets whizzed over my head, the rain kept pouring down. I found a soldier covered with mud and blood lying against a tree stump. He'd been hit in the legs. I put a tourniquet on each leg, but couldn't give him an IV because of the dirty conditions. I cleaned and dressed his wounds the best I could in the mud and rain. Lucky he had no broken bones. I gave him a shot of morphine and told him to try to relax, that he was A-OK. When the litter-bearers showed up, I told them to get the soldier an IV right away. Off they went. I started up the hill again.

Our battalion launched another mortar barrage on the upper part of the hill. We pounded the enemy mercilessly. Companies 1 and 2 were making great headway on their assault on the village, but at the cost of many good men. As our troops fought their way further up the hill, we passed trenches full of dead enemy bodies, muddy and bloody, mutilated. One of our BAR men said, "That's why we're here, to kill the damn Chinks."

It was now high noon. We still had plenty of enemy yet to snuff out of all the caves and bunkers. Going up the hill, I strained to pull my feet out of the sucking, sticky mud. In places it was nearly knee deep. The rain wouldn't stop. Elimination of the final Chinese holed up in the hill was left to our demolitions experts. They lowered time-fused satchel charges into the caves and into the peepholes of the bunkers, blasting them away. Our mortar men opened up with another pounding barrage.

We had only one hundred yards to go to get to the top of the hill. The remaining Chinese, in a last ditch effort, rolled grenades down at us. The shrapnel from one of them hit our radioman in the thigh. "Doc, I'm hit!" After taking care of him, I picked up the radio—some Chinese troops had made a run for it but were met by our automatic weapons fire. All were killed.

I made my way to the summit of the hill. Most of our company was already there. Hundreds of dead Chinese lay everywhere, as far as one could see. Unbelievable to witness. All I could think of was a lot of our good men had been lost. We had a lot of heroes that night, most of them dead.

CHAPTER 16

MONSOON RAINS

Besides the North Koreans, our other enemy these days was rain. This was monsoon season, and the rice paddies had turned into swamps. At times I couldn't see five feet in front of me. We were happy this was our third day without rain, but the mud was something else—it was everywhere. Our new troops were learning how to live in the mud and in soaking wet foxholes. The North Korean troops had been living with this every year. This was another day at the office for them, so to speak.

For the last two days, our troops had been fighting to take over a hill. I had patched up and tagged thirty-four WIA and tagged five KIA, just in our company. We were starting our advance again. It was 0600 hours and 87 degrees. This was *Operation Tunnel Rat*. Our action was timed to coincide with the last days of the rainy season. We'd flush the enemy out of flooded tunnels and bunkers. They would have been lying in wait in the water so long that their skins would be shriveled like prunes, and they would not be in the best of fighting condition.

The hill was big. It would take at least another day to reach the summit. The terrain was like a jigsaw puzzle and mud was knee deep in places. Danger was not just on the ground. The enemy had learned from us to suspend grenades from the trees, to be detonated by radio or by contact with trip wires as we passed. Our troops took an hour to go 150 yards. Everywhere we stepped was swampy, filthy mud.

Enemy automatic weapons fire erupted from above and we exchanged fire for about forty minutes. Our mortars laid down a white phosphorous smoke screen to block the enemy's view of us as we took to the higher ground. Slogging from bunker to bunker, our troops poured automatic fire and grenades into every enemy position they could find. One of our corporals opened fire to cover our platoon as we moved up. He withdrew from his position only to be shot as he attempted to rejoin us. I crawled across the muddy hillside to him, bullets flying overhead. He was dead. I tagged him KIA and dragged him down the hill to a safer place for the litter-bearers to fetch him. A litter jeep would take the body to our aid station. I worked my way back up the hill and found eight wounded who had been caught in a storm of machine gun fire. Four could get down the hill on their own. The radioman called for stretchers for the others and for another medic to help me.

Some of our flamethrowers got bogged down in the mud. They freed themselves and moved forward to take care of the trenches and bunkers, knocking them out one by one. Farther up the hill they found tunnels. The enemy's tunnels were complex, giving them not only a place to hide and fight, but a place to sleep, to plan, to train, and to store food and weapons. The troops called the enemy "tunnel rats." First the flamethrowers hit those tunnels, then dynamite—TNT—blew them all sky high, dirt and mud flying and rivers of unleashed rain water flowing down the hill.

The enemy attacked us from the higher ground no less than six times. We called for artillery to hit as close as fifty yards from our own position. We had been fighting all day and now it was late at night. The enemy made a last ditch effort to stop us, but they were running out of men and ammo. It was just a matter of time.

Our machine gun fire covered every avenue of approach as we worked our way higher up the hill. The darkness and the thick mud made our progress slow and hard. One enemy machine gun continued to cut all around us. Burp guns and small arms fire popped. We hugged the side of the slope, waiting for the fire to quiet down. The medics in the other platoon yelled for help. Our troops were trying to take out an enemy sniper, so I crawled on all fours through the mud, totally soaked in it. I got to the medics and had just started to bandage up the leg of one of their wounded when a bullet whizzed over my head from that sniper's rifle. It hit one of the litter-bearers. Blood flew everywhere. We rushed to him, but his throat was torn wide open and he bled to death within minutes. There was nothing we could do for him. It scared the wits out of me, thinking it could have been me, but I had to go on with my job. I tagged our man KIA. One dog tag went between his teeth, the other in my bag. The other litter-bearers put him on a stretcher. They'd have to wait to take the body down until our troops got that sniper. *War is hell!*

I made my way back through the mud, up the hill to my outfit. Orders had come for our battalion to take the hill at 0350 hours. In fifteen minutes our artillery and mortars would blast away at the hilltop. Like clockwork, all hell broke loose and night turned to day. Bayonets fixed, our platoon charged up the hill. Automatic weapons fire sprayed down. Our flamethrowers did their job, blasting away at the bunkers, setting them all ablaze.

We reached the top. Drag marks and blood trails indicated many of the enemy troops had left badly wounded. Dead bodies lay piled on top of each other as far as we could see. The surviving enemy had withdrawn down the backside of the hill and disappeared to fight us another day. After three days of fighting for the hill, we were damn glad it was over. My two aid kits were empty. This was the bloodiest battle of the month, but we handed out more punishment than we took. The climb down the other side of that muddy hill was as difficult as the climb up. I told the other medics, "I hope I never see another monsoon rain."

CHAPTER 17

THE STENCH OF BLOOD AND DEATH

"Doc, load up on medical supplies. I've got a funny feeling about this one."

This war was full of hills and valleys lost and taken over and over again. Twelve days ago, we had taken the hill we were on. Now we had orders to move out. Our company would take the lead and my squad would take the point—be the first to go. Our objective was a hill just to the north. As we left, a reserve battalion would move in behind us to cover the hill we had just captured.

By 0900 hours the day was already 90 degrees. To get to our objective, we would move through a small valley. On the left was a hill held by the ROK, the good guys of the Republic of Korea. Intelligence had it that the hill we wanted on the right was held by a North Korean force of two to three thousand troops with artillery and mortars. That hill had been lost and taken by the North Koreans five times. If we took that hill, we'd have control of both the hills as well as the valley between them.

Our squad leader gave us last-minute details. "If something happens, give our code word and tell Doc where you were hit." This was important when we were in tough battles getting a lot of wounded. If the wounded would yell out where they were hit, I could tell who to run for first. Gut injuries were first in line, then head wounds, then arms and legs. Every soldier carried a small first aid pack on his web belt so he or any other soldier could start basic care without waiting for me to arrive. Well, that's how it was all supposed to work, and sometimes it did.

Zero hour was here. As my squad led the way down our steep hill, some of our company behind us laid down a tremendous barrage of fire into the valley as a distraction. We had gone only fifty yards when the point man in our diamond formation saw something that didn't look right. He motioned to our leader and they discovered a small group of North Koreans waiting around for an opportunity for ambush. They were paying attention to our artillery fire and hadn't seen us. Our leader had our men circle around. As they got into place, on signal, they opened up with BARs, carbines, Garand rifles, and grenades. I went to make sure all ten enemy were dead. They were.

As our platoon got into the valley, a barrage of enemy artillery and mortars hit us. Bodies flew like Raggedy Ann dolls. I zigzagged from shell hole to shell hole, body to body, looking for wounded. In an hour, my litter-bearers and I must have taken care of ten to fifteen troops with shrapnel wounds. Only five of the thirteen in our squad had made it. We had to get closer to the base of our hill objective or we'd all be goners. The Lieutenant radioed for our heavy mortar units, hoping to buy us time.

Yelling for "Doc" was the order of the day. We were getting the shit pounded out of us. Eight men came in to replace the eight we had lost in our squad. Litter-bearers ran back and forth taking our wounded and dead back to the rear. The enemy was throwing everything at us but the kitchen sink. Smoke filled the valley. We made it to the base of the hill—I don't know how. We were to stay put and wait for all the platoons to move forward so we could attack as a unit. Our tanks, artillery, and mortar units moved up to work over the hill.

Orders came to move out. I stopped along the way to take care of wounded soldiers. By late afternoon, as I crawled slowly forward up the hill between enemy shell rounds, I noticed a terrible stench.

Battered bodies lay in the heat. Lucky for us, we didn't come across any minefields. The terrain was steep and rough, no cakewalk. We were taking a beating from small arms fire. Now and then the enemy dropped in a mortar round. The rumbling of both sides' artillery and mortars went on into the early evening. My new bulletproof vest was paying off. Adding to our troubles were the mosquitos. They were big and powerful and stung like hell.

We had to maneuver our way through an obstacle course, a jagged part of the hill. As we crawled over the rocks, the guy to the left of me fell. "Doc, I'm hit! It was burp gun fire—I know that sound anywhere!" I cut away his fatigue trousers and put a tourniquet high on his thigh. Two slugs had torn up his leg, shattering the bone. I gave him a shot of morphine and got four bayonets from nearby troopers to use as splints. Litter-bearers arrived and tagged him WIA. We needed a makeshift aid station. Our rear aid station was too far away for our worst cases.

Soon it would be dark. The LT had a couple squads go off to weed out some of the enemy still firing from bunkers above us. As they started up the hill, a volley of shells hurtled over our heads, whooshing into the valley behind us. One landed about twenty-five yards away from me. The concussion from the salvo lifted me off my feet. When I came around a few minutes later, my ears were ringing like hell. The dead and dying lay mangled and stacked everywhere. I'll never forget that scene. I checked my aid kits and heard a voice calling through the noise in my ears, "Doc, please help me!"

I made my way towards the sound. I found a trooper with both legs blasted off below the knees. He held his hands over his kneecaps trying to stop the bleeding. I yelled for the litter-bearers. I put a tourniquet high on each thigh to stop the rush of blood spattering everywhere. Another wounded called out and I yelled, "You're next, hang in there!"

I put tourniquets on, cleaned and dressed the two stumps, and gave our soldier a shot of morphine. "What do you think, Doc?" he asked. "I did the best I could for you. You're in a little shock, but you've got a good chance of making it." "Thanks, Doc, you're the best." The litter-bearers took him down the hill to a makeshift helicopter pad for an airlift back to MASH. As they disappeared, the sun vanished behind the mountains.

Our company hunkered down with the others, waiting for word on what to do next. We set up an aid station in an empty enemy bunker. One of our riflemen found a torn blanket and hung it over the entryway to block the light from the candle one of the litter-bearers had set out. We'd use the bunker for the more serious cases, like for the men who needed plasma right away. The rest would go straight down the hill to the rear aid station.

"Doc, Doc, over here!" I took two riflemen and the litter-bearers with me, crawling off to the right until we reached a huge shell hole. Inside was one of our riflemen holding onto his hand wrapped in a blood-soaked towel. Next to him was a BAR man. He had been hit in the shoulder and thigh. I had the litter-bearers help me take care of the men, and then take them down to the rear aid station. As I worked my way back to the aid bunker, streams of machine gun fire from both sides lit up the night.

The LT got a call on the radio. Battalion wanted all four companies to attack as one force—in fifteen minutes. I went out to check on our soldiers, passing out aspirin to a few with headaches. As I got back to the bunker, shells came flying over, blasting the hill above. They came so fast and furious the night was like day for the next thirty minutes. How the hell could anybody live through that.

A green flare went up, meaning move out. The clouds must have thinned because we could see a little better now. In our company, during night fighting like this we medics had our own codes to identify our men. For this battle, if a wounded called out for us we yelled *baseball*. Our wounded would yell back, *Yankees*. I kept a rifleman close to me, just in case.

Our troops engaged the North Koreans in a series of short but fierce firefights on our way up the hill. Our artillery and big mortars had inflicted severe damage, and the enemy ground troops' situation was getting worse. In another hour or so, most of the bunkers gun positions were knocked out. Our litter-bearers and I were hunkered down behind large rocks. We were under sporadic fire from a bunker above us. Then we heard, "Doc, I'm hit bad!"

We jumped up and ran toward the voice, going a zigzag course so as not to make a good target. Gunfire kicked dirt all around us. I yelled, "*Baseball!*" The voice called, "*Yankees!*" When we reached our wounded, he was doubled over, writhing in pain and gasping for breath. I pulled out my penlight and the litter-bearers held up a dark-colored towel to hide the light. The trooper was lucky—the bullet had gone through a fleshy part of his left side, touching no vital organs. I cleaned him up and the litter-bearers carried him down the hill.

Our troops were exhausted after sixteen sleepless hours of continuous fighting. They still had more to go. Someone had to knock out the remaining enemy in the bunkers just above. The LT asked for four volunteers, and I was to tag along. The terrain would be a bitch to climb. The four volunteers were experienced at climbing North Korean hills. I had gone on some raids with them before. They loaded up with everything—you name it, they had it. Sharpshooter rifles, BARs, ropes, TNT and other explosives. I carried the radio. I assigned everyone a number, so if they were hit they would call out their number plus *Yankees*. I was Number 5.

We made it up the hill some thirty yards without being spotted. Number 1, our leader, went to scout things out. Three bunkers were still in operation. Number 1 would take out the higher bunker, Numbers 2 and 3 would take out the other two. Number 4 would cover our exit. Off went the three men to set up units of TNT.

Sporadic fire came from above, and I hoped that wasn't the enemy shooting our guys. If they didn't return by the time set, orders were orders, and Number 4 and I would take off back down the hill without them. After a while, we heard a rumbling sound and took cover fast behind a big tree stump. Number 4 had his BAR cocked and ready to fire. The rumbling stopped. Number 4 called out, "*Baseball.*" Others answered, *Yankees.*" Up popped Number 1 followed by Numbers 2 and 3. "Let's get the shit out of here! The whole section is going up!" Just as we crossed into the safety of our side, the bunkers blew up into the sky.

All companies were to wait and attack in half an hour, but the battalion was hell-bent on giving the top of the hill one last blast from our big guns. For nearly twenty minutes they laid down an ear-splitting attack of artillery and mortar shells. Then we moved forward, and the battle raged for some three and a half hours through steep, rocky terrain cut up by trenches and small hollows. At sunrise the top of the hill appeared. Our troops kept climbing, taking out one bunker after another. The battle was intense, involving trench warfare, knives, bayonets, and hand-to-hand combat. The North Koreans fought vigorously, but our troops struggled and endured until the hill was secured. They cut down the straggling enemy running for the safety of the hills beyond. The entire battle for the hill had taken some twenty-three hours.

The North Koreans had suffered horribly, with their bunkers devastated and burning. Dead enemy covered the top of the hill, and the stench of blood and death filled the air. Rigor mortis would set in in about twelve hours, and when the bodies started to decompose, the smell would be almost unbearable. If we were going to stick around the area, our engineers would have to come in and dig huge holes and bulldoze the bodies into them.

We had our own share of dead and wounded. In our company alone we had twenty-one dead and forty-six wounded. Men died in pride and glory, but for the rest of us, life on the battlefield was a living hell. We had to shake it off, though. We knew there was more to come.

CHAPTER 18

EAGLE'S NEST

Scuttlebutt had it a special mission was being planned. It was late summer, and our battalion was setting up a perimeter in a big valley below the hill we had just won from the North Koreans. It was a successful end to a grueling and bloody four-day campaign. A reserve battalion had taken over the hill so our battalion could rest before heading up the valley to clash again with the North Korean Army. Our commander, a major, had us camping out in tents. While our worn troops went to sack out for the next eight hours, I had a chance to catch up on my rounds of sick calls—I still had some two dozen wounded to check up on from our last battle.

I had just finished my rounds and was about to hit the sack myself when the LT called me on the sound power phone at our medical tent. He said, "Doc, they asked if you'd go. They know you have mission experience."

"When do we leave?"

I was to report to the command post tent at 1600 hours (4:00 p.m.). I flopped on my cot to saw away, to get as much sleep as I could. An hour before reporting time I got up, filled my two aid kits plus my special medical shoulder bag, and put on my shoulder holster. I put my buddy—a .45 caliber pistol with silencer—in the holster and took off for the rendezvous.

Military police and their jeeps surrounded the CP area. Standing at the entrance of the tent was our battalion commander and a very distinguished man—a full bird colonel—plus two other men. The Major introduced the Colonel. "As of now he's running the show." The Colonel asked me to join him and two other men for the drive to a remote area about a mile back. The MP led the way. We approached two large tents and pulled up to the first one. Inside were tables marked by platoon numbers. After everyone was seated in their places, the Colonel introduced the two men with us at the head table. One was a South Korean interpreter who spoke four languages—Korean, Chinese, Japanese, and English. The other was a South Korean radioman. "And everyone here knows Doc. He'll lead the medical unit. I will be the team leader for this mission. I'll do my best to get you all through this alive."

The mission consisted of forty men. The 1st Platoon's men would be Team 1, and so on. Team 5 was our leader, our interpreter, our radioman, and me. The Colonel would be known only as Number 5—no rank or name. If the men needed a medic, they were to yell their team number and the word *medic*. Most of our time would be spent behind enemy lines blowing up bridges, railroad tracks, and ammo dumps.

The men were pumped up. "Let's kick some ass!" The Colonel pulled out a clicker and held it up. The men quieted down. He told them the clicker codes, then said, "Your knife is an essential tool in your personal kit, your battlefield buddy. Keep it in your leather sheath, and don't lose it. Tonight you'll sleep in the big tent next to this one. It has battle dress and gear for each of you, plus ammo. Are there any questions? If not, chow is waiting. Meet here after breakfast tomorrow, at 0900 hours, to rehearse. Dismiss!"

The next morning, Number 5 went over every little detail of the mission. Then we filed out to a large open field nearby. We medics stood on the sidelines as Number 5 put the teams through the wringer. He was a calm, cool leader. He had to convince the men that he knew the mission would succeed no matter what, and I think he did that. He drove each man hard, but drove himself as well.

After the men had a chance to rest, we were taken to our jump-off point. We passed through our battalion area and saw they were taking down the tents. They would follow us up the valley, hoping our team had done the job of making it easier for them to get through. Past the wire, we got into a diamond formation. Team 1 led with a point man. My Team 5 took up position in the middle. Team 4 was behind with a rear cover man. Both the point man and the rear cover man carried BARs. The enemy had a common tactic of hiding in the high weeds and bushes of no man's land and allowing our patrols to pass through, then opening fire from behind. For that reason, we had firepower at the rear and at the point.

We made our way safely through no man's land and the big valley. Our weatherman had predicted skies would be mostly cloudy through the night. Perfect for what we had to do. After zigzagging for some three hours, Number 5 gave one click and we stopped. He checked his compass to make sure we were headed the right direction. "Men, this is it. Our next objective is a dried up creek bed ahead." At two clicks, we took off.

Not long after, we heard one click again and stopped. Number 5, the interpreter, and two others went to check things out. Three enemy soldiers were sitting on boxes alongside the creek bed. Number 5 picked three of his weapons and knife experts. Within minutes the enemy soldiers were no more.

We crossed the creek bed and began hiking up a steep hill to reach the edge of a forest. No easy task. Each trooper had to carry pounds of ammo and explosives as well as his own equipment. It was dark now and at times we could only see about five to ten feet in front of us. When the last team made it up, Number 5 flipped open the lid to a leather pocket compass and cupped his hand around the instrument to see the glow of the bobbing needle pointing north. Having Army Ranger experience, Number 5 was an expert in navigating through dense dark forests like the one we were about to tackle.

We moved through the forest in a wedge formation with Number 5 in the lead. He whispered he heard movement ahead. We hit the ground, weapons cocked and ready to blast away in the dark. *Oh, shit! This is it!* Two large deer appeared, slowly making their way across our path, looking at us as they walked about six feet in front of our wedge. Once they disappeared, we took off again.

The winding, hilly terrain made our trip through the forest a nerve-wracking process. We feared suddenly meeting the enemy face to face. Our eyes searched the forest, our fingers often tense on the trigger. Sometimes the forest was so dark that to keep from being separated we had to hang onto the backpack of the man in front of us. After a few hours on the God-forsaken hill and a few more run-ins with our four-legged friends, the deer, we finally made it through the trees. Number 5 went over the plans one more time. "Listen up. I know it's damn hot, but keep your flak jackets on at all times. The train crosses the bridge and arrives at the warehouse around 2000 hours. After the ammo's unloaded we leave our rendezvous area at the base of this hill to get to our places. We'll set all charges, then meet back at the rendezvous area. Our interpreter and radioman will be there to cover our exit. Doc, you're with Team 1 at the bridge. I'll be with Team 2 at the warehouse. Let's go."

We heard the faint sound of a locomotive off in the distance. We had one hour and forty-five minutes to reach our rendezvous area in the valley below. A slight fog was rolling in from the stream that ran under the bridge—the bridge Team 1 was going to blow to smithereens. As the train come around the bend we watched the dim lights of the locomotive as it slowly made its way across the bridge and to the warehouse. Slipping and sliding, we worked our way down the rugged hill. Some areas were so steep we had to rappel using ropes.

At our rendezvous area, Number 5 stopped to radio home base to let them know we were at *Eagle's Nest*, our code name for the village, and that *the eagles were about to fly*, which meant we were about to go into action. He pulled out his field glasses to look over our target areas. To our left was the bridge and the stream leading to the warehouse. Behind the warehouse was a large rice paddy and to its right was the motor pool. Next to the motor pool were the living quarters. Dim lights shown over all four target areas. We saw no path to the bridge area, nothing but high weeds. The overhead doors of the warehouse closed. Ten of the enemy headed down the dirt road to the living quarters. They did not appear to have weapons.

My Team 1 took off for the bridge. Getting there was no easy task. Our move forward was measured by feet, not yards. We carefully made our own path single-file through all kinds of tall weeds and thorny bushes. We crawled to within twenty-five yards of the bridge and hid behind a rise that ran along the stream. Two guards, one at each end of the bridge, were sitting under the bridge lights on what looked to be old ammo crates. My team leader went to check things out. The stream was shallow, only about one to two feet deep and about twenty-five yards wide, but the current was strong. I was to go across the stream with one of our sharpshooters. There he'd have a better shot at the guard at the far end of the bridge.

The two of us went upstream some thirty yards so we could wade across without being seen or heard. The rest of our team hunkered down into position to cover for us, and our other sharpshooter set up to take out the closest guard. I had it easier than my sharpshooter buddy—he had to wade against the current while carrying an awkward, heavy load of equipment and ammo. He was over six feet tall, though, and weighed about 250 pounds, all muscle, so no problem. We got across and kept low in the high grass, the sharpshooter in the lead. He took position. At the designated time, I tapped his shoulder. Our guard and the other slumped over. We propped them up on their ammo crates so at a distance it would not be apparent they were dead. Our team went to work on the bridge, putting quarter-pound sticks and one-pound packs of dynamite onto the support beams. The explosives were linked together with detonation wires connecting to one timing device.

I watched Team 2, led by Number 5, enter the large warehouse. They would tape explosives to the boxes of ammo, flares, and weapons. Team 3 would set explosives to the heavy trucks, flat-bed trucks, and other kinds of vehicles in the motor pool, as well as to equipment and parts there. Meanwhile, Team 4's job was to quietly tape explosives to the barracks-like living quarters—inside were sleeping enemy troops.

My team finished up. One after the other we ran through the high grass to the bottom of the hill. Right behind us came Teams 2, 3, and 4, each making their five clicks-pause-two clicks signal as they approached. Our radioman and interpreter were waiting for us. We needed to beat a fast track to the top of the hill. The closer we got, the steeper it got. I thought we would never make it, but we did.

By now our battalion would be sitting a mile away from their target, which was the hill just to the right of the village. If all went well, the blast from the warehouse, motor pool, and living quarters would be their cue to get ready to attack the hill. Number 5 got home base on his radio. "The eagles are in the trees and flying south." We were in the forest and heading home.

The run back through the forest was as treacherous as it was coming in, but the impossible becomes possible when one is running for his life. Soon it would be dawn. We came to a cave where we could hide and get some much-needed rest, maybe even a catnap. We sprawled out on the dirt floor, but Number 5 said, "Don't get too comfortable, we leave in fifteen minutes." Suddenly the ground underneath us rumbled and rolled. "Get out in case it collapses from the blast!" Outside the cave we watched the sky light up and smoke rise a mile high. "Job well done! Now let's get the shit out of here!" With two clicks we were on the prowl again.

The sky began to get bright. At one click everyone ducked behind the trees. I kept my fingers crossed as we watched a North Korean patrol of seven cross within twenty-five yards in front of us. Number 5 waited to make sure they were well away from us, then gave two clicks to move out. So far luck was with us. In less than half an hour, we would be home free. We again heard one click and down we went. Three deer passed by. As we got close to the edge of the forest, Number 5 sent out two scouts. They found a couple enemy soldiers talking, their weapons leaning against a tree. Two of our top sharpshooters, silencers on, took off. After the enemy troops were out of our way, Number 5 radioed the coordinates of our position back to home base. "The eagles are out of the trees and heading for the nest."

With Team 1 leading the way, we took off single file down a hill that would give our guys plenty of scrapes, bruises, and more. We made it to our rendezvous and got into the waiting trucks and litter jeeps. A half mile away, we came across our battalion about to blast away that hill as planned. We wished them well and headed for our debriefing. We hoped our work behind enemy lines paid off. Number 5 radioed home base, "All the eagles are in the nest!"

CHAPTER 19

PRISONERS NO MORE

After two days of downpours the humidity was doing its part to make us miserable. That wasn't a monsoon rain—those go for weeks on end—just a good hard rain. Mosquitoes were out in force, swarming everywhere. They were big and there was no hiding from them. Some of the men had come down with malaria. They got chills, and fevers up to 103 degrees. I put them in their bunks and wrapped them in blankets.

At 0600 hours our sector of the MLR was quiet except for the troops complaining. I told them, "I'm a medic, not a chaplain. If you want to whine, go see the chaplain. He has a new supply of TS cards." The TS card had a fanciful meaning. When bad luck and distressing circumstances befell a soldier, he was advised to get his Tough Shit card punched.

Word had come down from Headquarters that our company had been tagged for a daylight raid deep into North Korean territory. Patrols were daytime and nighttime affairs for both sides. Ambush, reconnaissance, and combat patrols kept everyone on their toes. Any patrol meant hazardous duty. The enemy had taken ten of our troops as prisoners in a battle a few days ago. They were holding them in a village about five miles into North Korean territory, in front of our sector of the MLR. HQ said a daytime raid would be better than a night raid because we needed vehicles and didn't want them using headlights. The captain of our company would lead the raiding party. He needed two platoons. We would leave our MLR at 0830 hours, in an hour and a half. The code word for the raid was *Geronimo*. The password was *Jesse*, counter *James*. We medics made sure all were okay to go.

We went through the wire, down through our minefield, and through no man's land. Heading up the valley, I asked our lieutenant if the troops could stop ten minutes out of each hour for water and rest. I worried about heatstroke with the humidity and with the temperature being close to 90 degrees. With their fatigues and flak jackets, the troops would feel like it was 100 degrees plus. The forecast was for cloudy and 116 degrees by mid-afternoon. In any language, that's *hot*. The LT had to ask the Captain. He came back saying, "Captain said it's Doc's call, so okay."

Each platoon got into its own diamond formation. Our platoon covered the rear. We were about 150 yards behind the lead platoon. In between were three weapons carriers and five litter jeeps, with litter-bearers as well. We were loaded down with water, ammo, mortar rounds, and extra medical supplies.

It was a slow go. With our breaks for water and rest, five hours had gone by. Our target was less than an hour away. The Captain told the troops he didn't want any itchy trigger fingers, and they were to be especially watchful for booby traps as we patrolled along the steep, jagged ridges rising like knives above us. We had to work our way round those ridges. The terrain was rugged, with hidden caves in the high hills. The stifling 116 degrees as well as the annoying mosquitoes didn't make things any easier. All around us were insects and little creatures of many kinds, including scorpions. If those stung you, it would hurt for hours on end.

The Lieutenant came by when the troops were on a break. In combat conditions, we were not to address officers as "Sir" or by stating their rank because that might single them out for snipers or ambush. We called the Lieutenant "Peppy." The Lieutenant asked,

"Doc, are all the troops in our platoon okay?"

"Yes, they are, Peppy."

He raised his voice and told the men, "Watch the soldier to your left and the soldier to your right. Good luck!" As we headed up again toward our target, I thought, *Death is a part of life. War merely accelerates the process.*

The day wore on and the heat grew to oven-like intensity. During another break, Sarge, one of our squad leaders, asked me to look at two of his men who had blinding headaches from the heat and sun. As the men walked toward me, they looked like they were about to pass out. I had them lie on stretchers in one of our covered jeeps. I set each of them up with an IV. A litter-bearer watched over them as we went on up the path.

We were now approaching our target area, only about a thousand yards and two little ridges away. The Captain sent up a reconnaissance team to check things out. They made their way to the first little ridge overlooking a small village and radioed back to set up the mortar squad behind the second small ridge.

The sun beat down on us. It was the hottest part of the day. At 1630 hours (4:30 p.m.), my thermometer read 120 degrees, and we already had twenty-seven men who had overheated. The recon team ahead saw only six to eight soldiers wandering about the village. Most were probably in their huts, out of the blazing heat. If there was a time to go in, it was now.

After a quick conference with the two platoon leaders, the Captain said everything was a go. The raid had to be decisive and quick. First we had to wait until all fifty men and the medics of 1st Platoon were on the ridge overlooking the village, in place and ready. We four medics with 2nd Platoon were in reserve, stationed right behind the mortar position. When the Captain gave the signal, one of the men yelled, "Here, you bastards, have a belly full of good old American steel!" and the mortar guys let loose with a thundering ten-minute barrage.

One of the mortar men burned his hand. I put salve on it, then wrapped a soft gauze bandage around his palm and fingers. I told him to drink a lot of water and get some rest in the back of one of the litter jeeps. I'd be back later to rewrap his hand.

Following the mortar barrage, 1st Platoon went out with burp guns and BARs blasting away. The Captain was in the lead. Concussion grenades hit the enemy hiding in small ditches they had dug outside of the village area. Our machine gunners and snipers with their scopes picked off men wearing uniforms. They let the old men, women, and children flee to the hills beyond. Some gooks tried playing dead like possums, but they got it with the bayonets. Some were caught hiding in the huts, but our troops tossed in satchel charges, killing them all.

It was over in twenty minutes. When the dust and smoke settled, enemy bodies lay everywhere. Some of the village people came out and showed us where the ten prisoners were hidden. They were dirty, ragged, exhausted, and unshaven—but alive! We medics gave aid to the rescued prisoners as well as to all our wounded. We had a total of fifteen with leg, arm, and hip injuries, but no dead. Twenty-eight uniformed enemy from the village—dead.

I remembered what someone told me when I first came to this hellhole. One opponent lives and the other dies. As we made it back across our wire, I thought, This time our team lived, theirs died.

RESTRICTED

GENERAL HEADQUARTERS
FAR EAST COMMAND
MILITARY INTELLIGENCE SECTION, GENERAL STAFF

UNIFORM, INSIGNIA, EQUIPMENT
NORTH KOREAN ARMY

AUGUST 1950

RESTRICTED

CHAPTER 20

SEE YOU IN HEAVEN

It was our company's turn to go on a search and destroy patrol. Orders were to flush out the pesky enemy forces. Our battalion had just taken a big hill from the North Koreans after a two-and-a-half-day battle. It was a costly and arduous battle that fluctuated back and forth around the nearby villages, rice paddies, and fields. Eventually the North Koreans' resolve had broken, and our exhausted troops managed to clamber up the steep, rugged slopes to the top of the hill. Some of us had more work to do.

It was not just fighting the enemy that had worn our troops out. The weather and terrain, too, proved as much of a burden. The mid-summer temperature had hit a blistery 107 degrees, and the hill had cliffs, slopes, and ravines that even most of the mountain goats stayed away from. Our battalion had paid heavily. We lost 125 heroes. Out of the four companies, ours had taken the biggest hit. We lost fifty-one men—three medics out of sixteen, and forty-eight men out of 258. But, with only two days to rest, regroup, resupply, and train our replacement troops, our company was on the move again.

For our replacements, this would be their first engagement with the enemy. During our two days of rest, we "old" medics did our best to prepare our three new medics for what to expect. My last words to them were, "It can get deadly in the blink of an eye. We're fighting an enemy that is ruthless and acknowledges no rules in warfare. So keep your butts down, and good luck."

Our objective was a village about a half mile on the other side of no man's land. We were to meet at the MLR at 1100 hours. Each platoon had four medics plus eight litter-bearers. The code word for the mission was *Jackpot* and the password to cross the wire was *thunder*, counter *bolt*. As we reached no man's land, each platoon got into a diamond formation, with its medics and litter-bearers in the middle. The Captain and 1st Platoon took the lead. The other platoons followed, staying twenty-five yards apart.

The sun's rays beamed down, baking everything on the ground. It was getting hotter by the hour. At noon it was 110 degrees in the shade, and the bulletproof vests we all wore made it feel like 120. We were fighting two enemies again—the North Koreans and the weather. I told our new medics to make sure they and our troops drank water on the hour. If anyone needed salt tablets, we had them.

The village we called *Jackpot* was now only about one hundred yards away. It was very quiet, and I could sense something was in the air—garlic. The Koreans ate a lot of it. At times you could smell a village a mile away, the odor was that strong.

The Captain, looking through his field glasses, saw the village had a very large area of rice paddies, about the size of a football field. We would have to go through the paddy area or around it. The Captain sent out a recon patrol of eight men to look things over. Row upon row of paddies were arranged in slightly sloping terraces draining downward. A soldier on one end of a terrace would be higher than a soldier on the other end. The terraces were like big, wide, wet stairs going down.

As the recon patrol got about fifty yards into the paddies, about halfway to the village, the Captain had the 1st and 2nd Platoons fan out and start their advance. Suddenly the sky opened up. Not with rain, but with mortar shells coming from the village. Mortars landed all around the recon patrol, killing all the guys instantly. The two advancing platoons dove into the paddies for cover. The enemy had sprung their trap. Our guys were like ducks on a pond. The mortar barrage lasted about ten minutes, then came the automatic weapons fire along with machine gun fire sweeping back and forth. That sure stopped the Captain's advance. From a distance, we could see our men in the first two platoons falling like flies. We heard them yelling, "Doc... I'm hit, Doc…Please, Doc over here!"

I don't know how long they were pinned down—seemed like a lifetime. I knew one thing, we medics had to get to the wounded fast. By now 3rd and 4th Platoons had set up their mortar units. Once their barrage on the village started, we would do our best to get to our wounded. All we needed was a rifleman each for protection. LT said, "Take your pick." I told the three new medics to keep their butts down, this was their time to shine. "Let's Go!"

As we took off for different areas of the rice paddies, we heard the Lieutenant rallying his troops with shouts of encouragement. Sporadic mortar rounds were still coming from the village. Our men crawled slowly through the rice paddy as though oblivious to mortar shells and sniper fire all around them. The men in 3rd Platoon stirred themselves and began their advance. By now there were plenty of shell holes to take cover in. Despite our heavy casualties, there was to be no letup in our advance. A burst of our mortar fire scored a direct hit on one of the enemy's mortar emplacements.

I made my way up to one of our wounded. He'd taken a bullet to the stomach that had thrown him flat on his back in the paddy. Fortunately, he was graced by unconsciousness. He bled to death in a few moments. I tagged him and moved over to two more wounded. One had a bullet nick his neck near the shoulder. The other was holding his side from a bullet gash near his rib. Neither was wounded seriously or bleeding heavily. I tended to both and moved on.

I saw a soldier get shot and ran over to him, but he, too, was on his back in the wet of the rice paddy, staring blankly at the sky. Blood soaked his fatigue pants and jacket, his hands clutching his abdomen were red. He coughed, spraying blood into the air. "Kill me!" he pleaded as I reached into my aid kit for field dressing. I turned and looked at him. He closed his eyes and whispered, "See you in heaven." The rifleman protecting me said, "Doc, there was nothing you could do."

As we crawled upward, we couldn't go anywhere without climbing over a body or a piece of body. Shells ripped off limbs, tossing flesh and leaving ragged stumps disgorging blood. Men went sailing into the air, others were simply torn apart. The smoke from the enemy's mortar shells carried the smell of burning flesh. Soldiers fell in clusters screaming, then went silent.

Seeing that the situation had become desperate, our squad leader grabbed his burp gun and charged the enemy, firing his gun from the hip, moving forward through a hail of bullets. Immediately he was hit by machine gun fire and fell into the rice paddy. He scrambled back up and continued advancing, spraying bullets as he went. Mortar shells fell all around. He was hit a second time and fell, seriously wounded. Once more he staggered to his feet and continued toward the enemy. He was hit a third time and went down. He did not get up. I crawled over and saw there was nothing I could do. He was one brave hero. One of the litter guys tied him down on a stretcher to take him back to our makeshift aid station some one hundred yards to the rear.

Our journey through the rice paddies was slow and dangerous. Our mortars shells had silenced two more of the enemy's mortar emplacements. Terrain around and in the village made it obvious this was not going to be an easy battle. It was now 1530 hours (3:30 p.m.), and the temperature was 113 sizzling degrees. We'd have a bitter battle to reach and hold the village. We medics had to get the wounded out of the baking heat fast.

One of the top sergeants of our platoon, armed with his BAR, set up on a nearby paddy and blasted away at the village entrance. In between blasts, other troops hurled phosphorous grenades. At the entrance of the village was a machine gun emplacement. One of our corporals stood up and headed straight for it, shooting and throwing hand grenades. He knocked it out, killing all the men inside. The 1st and 2nd Platoons launched an assault, charging with fixed bayonets. The other platoons followed as backup. Once in the village, we found hordes of North Korean troops dead, but no village people. They must have been sent to the hills.

The battle was successful, but we had eighty-two casualties— twenty- seven dead and fifty-five wounded. We counted over 350 dead North Koreans and found a substantial amount of equipment. Our troops were exhausted from hours of non-stop action. The fighting had been bloody and strenuous, demanding the utmost in physical strength, endurance, and raw courage.

After an hour of mopping up the village, we headed back to home base with all of our wounded. I told our new medics they had all done a super job. But all I could think about was the men who had died.

Library of Congress, Prints and Photographs Division

CHAPTER 21

BLOODBATH

This was our fifth day of fierce fighting to take complete control of a huge valley. Our main objective was a hill on the right. We had only another thousand yards to go to reach the base of the hill, but it would not be a cakewalk. Sixteen days ago we secured the hill on the left, halfway through the valley. After four hours of non-stop fighting, it was finally ours. Those who made it out alive had the scars to show for it. Was the price of that victory worth it? Twenty killed and sixty wounded in our company alone. We lost three super medics. One of them was a buddy medic in my platoon. He was giving aid to a wounded. I was heading for him, but my friend got there first. A sniper got both him and the wounded.

Again our battalion would take the lead. My thermometer read 96 degrees at 0900 hours, hot and humid. Our battalion's big guns laid down a fierce barrage, warming things up for my 1st Platoon to assault the hill. The 2nd and 3rd Platoons would follow and 4th Platoon would stand in reserve. As we moved forward, mortars came down all around, bodies and parts flying everywhere. As I was putting a battle dressing on one of our wounded, I heard a mortar coming in and ducked. Next thing I knew, I was on the ground and my platoon leader, Sarge, was shaking me, "Doc, Doc, are you okay? We thought you were dead, too!" The wounded had been killed instantly. I looked at my helmet and at my bulletproof vest. They were riddled with shrapnel.

"Doc, Doc, up here!"

"Thanks, Sarge, I'll be okay." I shook off the haze and crawled up the hill toward the cry. The powerful sounds of a BAR echoed ahead of me. A BAR weighs about 16 pounds and the bullets are almost as big as a finger. For some reason, the BARs always seemed to be carried by little guys, their vest pockets or web belts loaded with heavy ammo. The only black soldier I remember seeing with our units was a guy about five feet tall who carried a BAR. He must have been tough.

I found our wounded man had died. The trooper and three others had been killed by one horrible explosion. It was almost impossible to crawl anywhere and not touch a wounded or dead. I left the tagging of the dead to the litter-bearers.

One of our company's squad leaders caught up with me. As we advanced up the hill, mortars came down like rain. We were also receiving machine gun fire from bunkers just above us. The hill was damn steep, and the terrain was a bitch. We'd take one step up and slide two steps back. The Chinese fired round after round on us before our guys found their artillery position and silenced them. Then we got pinned down by two machine gun emplacements. Lucky for us, there were a lot of large craters to hide in. The squad leader said, "Doc, stay put. I'll be right back." He took off running and jumping from one crater to another until he got close enough to the emplacements to hurl grenade after grenade, putting both guns out of commission. Now we could advance up the hill. When Sarge and I caught up with him in a crater, I told him, "That was one gutsy move!" He said, "Something had to be done. Besides, Doc, you risk your life for us when we get hit."

"But that's my job, you didn't have to do that."

"Come on, Doc, let's get the shit to the top."

We took off again. We were between two mountains and the sun had gone down behind one. For the next hour the deafening sounds of automatic weapons fire penetrated the air. The Chinese bunkers were really tough. The only thing that could take out those emplacements were our tanks with their 90 mm, high velocity, armor-piercing shells. So our company leader, the Lieutenant, thought he'd surprise the enemy. He radioed for our six tanks to move forward and blast the upper and middle parts of the hill. For the next hour or so, blast away they did. Shells flew over our heads, some landing as close as one hundred yards in front of us. For us, they couldn't blast fast enough. For five days we had been getting the shit kicked out of us. We were ready to finish this mission.

Word came for all platoons to resume their climb to the top. With the moon going in and out between clouds, I could see about twenty to thirty yards in front of me. With a sharpshooter shadowing me, I headed upward. Bullets came raining down on us from every direction. We heard a faint cry for help off to the left. We found two wounded soldiers from another squad lying out in the open. I'd have to go some twenty-five feet to reach the men and then get them to a crater about ten feet away. I told my shadow to cover me.

"Doc, you'll never make it."

"If I don't, they'll both die."

"Okay, Doc, on three." As he yelled three, I ran zigzagging forward. Just as I got to the men, bullets came zipping in. I hit the ground and crawled behind a pile of rocks. We had to get rid of that sniper. I yelled out that on the count of three, I was going to throw my helmet out into the open. When the enemy fired at it, our sharpshooter would see the flashes from the muzzle of the weapon. Our sharpshooter had better be ready! At three, out went my helmet. Our sharpshooter zoomed in on the flash. With one shot, he hit that sniper, who dropped and rolled down the hill.

One at a time, I dragged the wounded into the crater. The sniper had hit them in the legs. I yelled for my buddy medic and two litter-bearers. We spent close to thirty minutes giving aid. Then the litter-bearers took the men down the hill to our makeshift aid station.

Our Lieutenant radioed over to Sarge, "This is day six now. Let's end it. Move out." Men were being hit at a dizzying rate. One of our guys felt a machine gun bullet crease his fatigues high inside the thigh. He undid his pants, pulled them down, and inspected the damage. "I thought the damn Chink got the family jewels!"

Sarge yelled, "That's nothing to write home about! Get those damn pants up and catch up with the rest of the guys."

The shelling began to taper off, but every now and then a few Chinese would pop up, spray us with their burp guns, and then duck back down in their trenches. Sarge crawled over to me. "We don't stop until we hit their trenches. For the rest of the way up, you stay close to the Lieutenant's group and my two shadows. We're moving out and up at 0100." That meant six minutes from now. Our big guns from the battalion were going to light up the night with fireworks.

At 0100 sharp came one of the loudest sounds I'd ever heard. Hundreds of rounds of artillery flew over us, pounding the middle and top parts of the hill, picking up where the tankers had left off in the evening. While our artillery bombarded the enemy above, we took off like jackrabbits, running and jumping from crater to crater. Even under all that fire, the enemy sent burp gun rounds splattering in front of our platoon, bouncing like ping pong balls, throwing dirt and pieces of rock everywhere. We took a beating from those flying rocks. I had my hands full patching up troopers with gashes on their faces, arms, hands and legs.

I heard crying from a crater a few yards from me. Dead soldiers lay everywhere. I could not get used to seeing so many dead and dying soldiers. Here I was looking at the raw flesh and bones of an eighteen-year-old from our squad. His right arm and shoulder were nearly detached from his body and I knew he was beyond help. I gave him a shot of morphine, told him that was the best I could do. He said, "Doc, would you hold me?" I gathered him up, then he squeezed my hand and let go. I set him down carefully and yelled for the litter-bearers to come tag him. I had to move on.

I found we had another problem. Besides bullets and mortars hitting our troops, we had dehydration. I had warned the troops over and over to take their salt tablets and drink plenty of water. Dehydration can affect the performance of soldiers or even incapacitate them. The night was humid, ninety-six degrees and holding.

We were now about two hundred yards from the enemy trenches and bunkers. Some platoons were still under intermittent fire, mostly sniper fire, but our area was quiet. The LT came up with a game plan. Once our sharpshooters silenced some of the enemy trench line soldiers, our platoon would move up. The Lieutenant picked four of his top men to do the job. Our radioman was to go along. The Lieutenant asked me if I'd go, just in case.

We worked our way up the steep terrain to within twenty-five yards of the enemy's trench lines. Our four sharpshooters zeroed in on four targets, eliminating them and leaving a gap in enemy lines. They radioed back—job done. Our platoon quickly and quietly moved up the hill in the dark, bayonets and knives ready. The rest of the company caught up with us. One of our top men crawled up and over the enemy's bunker with a bag of grenades and started throwing them up and down the trench lines. Three others joined in and the fire grew intense. All was chaos, smoke, and dead bodies.

Getting over the enemy's trench line heralded the start of a more dangerous phase of the battle. Our men from all platoons howled like Indians on the warpath in the old Wild West. The battle was ferocious and at close quarters with hand-to-hand combat. Our troops used a commando-type trench knife. The seven-inch blade could inflict maximum damage. It was hell every step of the way. With a sharpshooter in front and one behind me, I worked my way through the trench, stepping on dead Chinese. Bullets flew over our heads and grenades blasted away in the bunkers. I heard another cry for help, "Doc, up here!" We found a trooper lying on top of five dead enemy he might have killed. I reached down and my hands became covered with blood. No response, no pulse, no breathing. I tagged him KIA and noted a Bronze Star for his actions.

The chill of death hung in the hot air as our troops went along the enemy's trenches raising havoc. Our demolitions and explosives guys placed charges on the bunkers for maximum effect, destroying them one by one. Dead Chinese lay everywhere, many killed by bayonet or trench knife. A bullet zinged by me. Miraculously, I wasn't hit. We found a soldier in one helluva bad way. A mortar had landed near and he had gone flying. His legs, arms, and face were full of shrapnel, blood everywhere. His fatigues had been ripped almost completely off. Suddenly the force of a blast threw me down on top of the soldier. A mortar had landed nearby. I got up and found the soldier was dead.

The sun finally came up over the mountain and dawn greeted our weary troops. We still had another tier of trenches and bunkers to get through before reaching the top. Our platoon used ropes to lead an assault up a rock face so sheer and treacherous that the Chinese barely bothered defending it. At the top, the Lieutenant and some of his top men fanned out with bayonets fixed, and at close range engaged the last of the Chinese with everything they had.

The hill was now ours. The sun shone on the horrible bloodbath that had transpired during the night. My uniform was full of blood. Mutilated bodies of hundreds of enemy soldiers littered the area. I was damn glad to see that most of the two squads I had covered had made it, but we had lost four men. The past six days had been a nightmare. We spent four hours tending to our wounded and dead. More Chinese were killed during mop up as we found them pretending to be dead, waiting to jump up and get us. At high noon I helped our litter guys take the last of our dead on stretchers down to the bottom of the hill to waiting litter jeeps. One of the drivers yelled, "Doc, how was it?"

I yelled back, "It was hell!"

CHAPTER 22

LUCK OR FATE

We had just won a series of breathtaking victories. Our men had fought gallantly against great odds and at high cost—we lost 256 men. In one battle, our battalion of 1,000 men was up against some 10,000 North Korean troops. In another, we were pitted against about 15,000 Chinese troops. Our troops were well trained and disciplined and we had good planning and strategy, plus a lot of firepower. The enemy often seemed helter skelter and depended on overpowering us with waves of charging bodies.

We were now on a hill almost 2,000 feet high. The Chinese wanted it badly and were willing to die for it. Our battalion commander was a lieutenant colonel. My company commander was a captain, my platoon leader was a first lieutenant. All three were damn good men. Our troopers, medics included, would go to hell and back for them—and we did.

We had seen many cases of combat fatigue. We sent them all back to our BAS. Some men just couldn't take all the stress that came with war. Besides the horrors of combat, we had other challenges to deal with. Korea had those mosquitoes and flies, some as big as hornets, also huge rats, poisonous snakes, and other assorted unpleasant critters. Today we had heat and humidity along with those damn assorted bugs and critters. Just another day in hell.

I was with my buddy medic stocking up our aid kits when we heard a knock on the door of our bunker and one of our squad leaders came in. After our last battle and after serving over a year "in this hellhole," he had enough points to rotate back to the States. "I just left the Lieutenant's bunker to thank him for being a good Joe," he said. The Lieutenant had been holding 120,000 Korean won for him, money from playing craps and poker over the year. He said, "I got a three-hour flight this afternoon from Seoul to Tokyo, then a fifteen-hour flight back to the States, then home! I want to thank you guys for saving my life. Thank all the other medics, too." As he left our bunker he yelled, "Keep your asses down!" Then off he went down our back slopes to a waiting jeep for the long ride to Seoul. He was one lucky guy.

We needed to earn at least 40 points before we were eligible to go back to the States. Points were assigned each month by if we fought in combat or by how close we were positioned to the front lines. One month on the front lines earned four points. A trooper could get points for other reasons, too, like if he got a medal.

We were about to leave for our morning rounds when we got a call on our sound power phone. Our platoon leader, the Lieutenant, said Headquarters had new intelligence reports. If the Chinese attacked our front line tonight, they'd probably be in our company's sector, and we were short of men. In Korea, almost every unit I was in was under strength. Sometimes we had as few as five men to a squad instead of around ten. After our last two battles, our battalion of 768 men left included only 32 medics instead of the 45 needed for that many men. We did have some new troops brought in, but scuttlebutt was that we would get more replacement troops as well as more medics in two to three weeks. We had heard that before!

My buddy medic and I took off for our sick call rounds. I covered Area 1, named code Red, as well as Area 2, code White. The other medic covered Area 3, code Blue, and Area 4, code Green. I was giving out pills and patching up old wounds in one of the forward bunkers when one of our squad leaders came over. "Doc, two bunkers down we've got a trooper in bad shape. Can you take a look?"

I took the trooper's temperature, then asked his buddies to find a bucket, some ice that had been brought in from the BAS, and about eight large towels. I gave him two quinine tablets to reduce his 103.5 degree fever. He had malaria. I wrapped a towel around the ice and put it over his forehead and put another on the back of his neck. His buddies took off his shoes and socks and stripped him down to his skivvies. Then I laid iced towels over his whole body and covered him with his blanket. "I'm playing it safe," I told him. "I'm sending you down to the BAS. They can take better care of you there."

I had to finish my rounds. In one bunker I cleaned up a deep gash in a trooper's forehead, a wound from our last battle. His buddies asked if I'd like a cup of joe, but I said, "I don't drink coffee." Then, just to be sociable I said, "Okay, just a sip." They pulled out four battered cups.

"What kind of coffee is this?"

"It's chicory. Do you like it?"

"It tastes like shit!"

They laughed, "Yeah, but it's all we got. Hope you live through it!"

As I left, they yelled, "Doc, you're a good sport!"

With my sick calls finished, I headed back to the aid bunker. I asked my buddy medic there who didn't drink coffee either, "What in the hell is this chicory coffee? I just had a sip of that damn stuff."

"Yeah," he said, "I heard it's wicked."

"It's one of those days," I said. My buddy medic knew what I meant. We medics spent a lot of our slow time—when the enemy wasn't attacking us—probing wounds for bullets and shrapnel as well as stitching up ripped flesh. We took care of lesser wounds. I had six different sizes of tweezers and scissors and three different sizes of a boring tool that looked like a flat fingernail file with bristles at the end. I used those boring tools to ream out wounds where the bullet had gone clean through, to clean out the hole. Sometimes a soldier would scream and then I had to tell him to shut up, especially if it was night because the sound would really carry. We didn't want the enemy shooting at us.

At noon we got another call from the LT. Our whole battalion was on full red alert, and we were to prepare for an all-out attack by the Chinese. Hearing the siren, we took off for our assigned areas on the forward slopes. I checked out some of the line troopers. I reminded them to yell out—if at all possible—their area code color if wounded. Many of the guys were spouting off, angry at the Chinese, filled with hate and hungering for revenge for killing their buddies in the last battle. I told them, "Don't let your anger get yourselves or your buddies killed."

A new young line trooper asked, "Doc, why do we have two dog tags?" I told him they should never be taken off, even when showering—if he ever got a chance to shower. One tag was for us medics to put between his teeth in case he was killed, and the other we or the litter-bearers would give to Graves Registration later. The tags should match. He was probably sorry he had asked.

I headed back up to our aid bunker to meet up with my buddy medic, who had only been with our unit for a short time. While packing up our aid kits and aid bags for the battle, I told him I'd learned not to get too close to any of the troopers or the other medics in my unit. One minute you have a close friend, the next minute they're gone—dead. I was remembering the troopers and medics we had lost.

We went over our game plan with the litter-bearers to make sure we were all on the same page for the upcoming battle. I said, "Remember, if we're going to pull this off, it's going to take teamwork. Make sure you each have two canteens of water because it's 96 degrees out there and the humidity is just as bad." As our litter guys were leaving, one of them yelled, "Doc, don't forget the insect repellent!" I told him a litter jeep was on its way with five cases.

I headed down the trench to give aspirins to one of our troopers with a migraine. A squad leader, a veteran of numerous battles, called out to me. He was a little nervous because he knew what to expect, but told me some of the new front line replacements were scared because they didn't know what to expect. I told him he and the others wouldn't be human if they weren't a little scared. As he took off up the trench I said, "Hang in there!" I, too, was a little scared, however I didn't want anyone to know because my job was to pump the men up, not be scared along with them.

Darkness fell. The LT called to say the Chinese were forming in a staging area in front of our sector, about a half mile up the valley. It looked to be a force of about 25,000, and we should prepare for an attack soon. I hung up and told my buddy medic, "Things could get a little dicey because the two of us have to cover some three hundred yards of platoon trench line between us. We've done it before, we can damn well do it again."

We wished each other good luck. As we stepped out of the bunker and into the sweltering heat and humidity, I noticed the thermometer on our bunker door read 105 degrees. I told myself, *Your training and experience have prepared you for this moment. Keep your head.* Then in the distance I heard the sound of truck motors. The waiting was over. All hell broke out. So many shells landed on our hill that the ground seemed to sway back and forth. Enemy mortars and artillery rounds zeroed in on us, hitting us with pinpoint accuracy. Every part of our company's trench line was catching hell. Three to four hundred mortar and artillery shells must have landed up and down our sector of the front line. After forty-five minutes of trying to blast us off our hill, the enemy got eerily quiet. I knew that was the cue for waves of old men, women, and children to begin charging us. Then the regular Chinese troops would come, hoping we'd be low or out of ammo.

True to form, coming up the steep, rugged terrain of our hill was the first wave of people. Our platoon leader had his troopers open fire, not knowing if it was against old people and children or against Chinese regulars. Then we heard sporadic fire and knew a few soldiers were intermingled with civilians, making sure none of them turned back. We heard the screams and cries of the dying while others kept coming up our hill under fire. Now we started getting a lot of automatic weapons fire. That was a sure sign the Chinese regulars were coming at us in force now.

Bullets hit off our forward bunkers. One of our squad leaders yelled, "Doc! Their snipers are damn good! They got huge night scopes. They aim for the neck, between our helmets and flak jackets, so keep your head down because we're gonna need you tonight!"

They were all over our hill by the thousands. The enemy's mortars and artillery shells fell like hail. LT called for our mortar and artillery. Within minutes, rounds from our battalion units were flying over our heads. All front line and tank machine gun units blasted away at anything that moved up our hill. I heard a loud cry, "Doc, it's Sarge in Area White!"

I made my way through the stacks of dead Chinese bodies that littered our trenches and finally found Sarge. One of our line troopers was holding his head up, pressing a small ammo towel onto his forehead. The towel was soaked with blood. A buddy with a BAR fired away at the oncoming enemy. We pulled Sarge up against the trench wall. I leaned his head back so I could work on him in the flashes of light from incoming shells. I told the line trooper to yell for the litter-bearers as I pulled the towel away and saw the gash made by flying shrapnel. Sarge asked, "Doc, how bad is it?"

"I've got everything under control. You've got a big gash." I got the bleeding stopped and put zinc oxide salve over the wound, taped it closed, and bandaged it. "Sarge, you're going to need a stitch job to close that gash. The litter-bearers will get you down to the surgeons at BAS. I can't give you morphine because it's a head wound." I tagged him WIA. The litter guys arrived and I gave them two aspirins to give to Sarge in case he got a headache. As they headed down the back slopes, I heard "Doc, Area Red!" and took off, incoming mail landing all around.

The scene was total destruction and confusion. The trench line had partly collapsed, and piles of dirt were everywhere. "Over here, Doc!" I crawled around and found three troopers sprawled out and half-covered in dirt. A mortar had gotten them. One of our BAR men showed up to cover for me, then four litter-bearers appeared. I yelled, "Who's the worst off?" One had leg wounds. Another had leg and arm wounds. The third yelled he had a stomach wound. I yelled back, "Don't move. Hang in there."

Two of the litter-bearers held large bandages around the man's stomach so I could tape them together. I gave the trooper a shot of morphine and tagged him WIA. I did not put anything on his tag about him not wearing his flak jacket. That was between him and me. The litter-bearers rushed him down the back slopes. The other two litter-bearers had uncovered the other wounded and put tourniquets on them. I tended to them and the litter-bearers took them away one at a time.

I headed toward another cry for help. A trooper was screaming about how he had seen two of his buddies hit dead-on by mortar shells, their bodies blown into a million pieces. Once I had him calmed down, I heard another scream. "Doc, Area White!" Crawling over more piles of dead Chinese, bullets zipping overhead and mortar rounds landing all over our hill, I zigzagged my way over. I found one of our machine gunners firing away. He pointed downward. In between bursts, he yelled that his assistant gunner had fallen over and had not moved. I pulled the man up from his slumped position and saw the huge hole in his forehead. I checked his pulse, but I knew he was dead. I leaned his body against the trench wall and covered him with a small tarp. Another trooper took over as assistant.

By midnight our troops had killed scores of enemy, but they kept coming up the hill by the hundreds, if not thousands. I didn't think they would ever stop. The battle seesawed back and forth for another hour or so. Throughout, the temperature hovered around 100 degrees. I tended four head injuries, three abdominal wounds, and two sucking chest wounds, which is where a bullet hole lets air get sucked into the chest cavity during breathing and can cause a collapsed lung. A couple hours later, so many men were crying "Doc" that there was no way just two medics could get to them all. Some would surely die.

A yell for help came from in between Areas Red and White. The trooper was badly wounded. I put his head in my lap. He cried out, "Doc, I'm gonna die!" And then he did. He looked to be about seventeen. On my way in to Area Red I stopped by one of our BAR positions. The trooper yelled through the noise, "How's it going, Doc?"

"We're slugging it out. If this was a boxing match, it'd be the ninth round out of twelve." Shells whistled over our heads.

"Doc, as long as you can hear the shells coming, you're still alive!"

A few yards up into Area Red I heard, "Help, Doc!" I found a trooper pointing, "Over there!" Leaning against his position was his buddy. A bullet had gone right through his throat. He had probably died instantly. "Doc, duck!" Up jumped four Chinese within ten feet of us. The trooper fired off a whole magazine clip from his carbine, killing all four. I gave him two thumbs up and then tagged his buddy.

A few yards farther up, I found a trooper with an arm and a face wound. While I taped him up, a mortar landed a little ways down the trench, the force of the blast knocking me flat on my ass, aid kit and all. My ears were ringing. Trench dirt was everywhere. Lucky for me and the wounded, the blast was at the bend of the trench line. Shrapnel had flown upward, not toward us. Once I shook the cobwebs out of my head, I pushed the dirt off us and went back to taping up the wounded.

"Doc, Area White!" I found a trooper lying in the trench. He had taken shrapnel to his ankle. I pulled him up against the trench wall. I looked up, and coming toward us was a Chinese carrying a burp gun. As he stepped over some of his own dead, I pulled my .45 out of its holster and fired two rounds in his direction. Down he went, right on a pile of his dead friends. I think I peed my pants.

Our trooper said, "Doc, I owe you a beer!"

"I'll take you up on that someday." That was one of my more frightening experiences. After taping up the trooper's ankle, I continued on. Further down the trench, a mortar round had hit in front of a line trooper's position. I found pieces of him everywhere. I picked up what looked to be part of a hand, wrapped it in gauze and put it in one of my aid kits to be sent down later to Graves Registration. With luck, maybe tomorrow we would find his dog tags.

Parts of our trench line in Areas Red and White had sustained direct hits from big mortars. One of our squad leaders came running up holding a small towel to the side of his head. "Doc, can you help me?" He fell to the ground. I leaned him up against the trench wall. Blood gushed from a good-sized hole where a piece of shrapnel must have hit him. Shrapnel, even the small pieces, were nasty bastards. I made an attempt to bandage the man up, but to no avail. He must have already lost a lot of blood. I put his head in my lap and held him a minute until he died in my arms. As I tagged him KIA, I thought, *War is the shits!*

I went up and down Areas Red and White tending to our wounded. Even in the early morning hours, the heat and humidity were as much of an enemy as the diehard Chinese troops. The LT went up and down our trench line as well, giving encouragement to his troopers. Dozens upon dozens of Chinese jumped up and over our trenches. At times they were so close we could easily have spit on them, but waiting for them on our back slopes and having a field day were our BAR men.

Then we heard the sounds of bugles. The Chinese had finally conceded defeat. Those who were left retreated down the hill. Our hail of artillery and mortar fire landed among the enemy as they crossed into the valley below and faded into the hills beyond to lick their wounds. All was over at 0530 hours. Our battle-weary soldiers could now rest and recuperate, at least for a little while. This had been the most savage fighting imaginable. There's no morality in warfare. You kill, no matter who it is…even old men, women, and yes, even children.

My buddy medic came by and we looked at the hillside in front of us littered with thousands of bodies. The smell of death was strong. We had won the battle for the hill, but at a terrible cost. When we got back to our aid bunker some ten and a half hours later, I had time to think, and I concluded that what had helped me the most was to stay calm amid the chaos. But my thoughts would turn from time to time to the horrors I had experienced. I knew I would remember for as long as I lived how thousands of the enemy came at us. I would remember our men that died. I had had my share of close calls and I could not believe that I was still alive and unscathed. I wondered, was it luck, or fate?

CHAPTER 23

BAYONETS AND KNIVES

It wasn't unusual for me to go on two missions in one day. I had returned from a night patrol at 0345 hours. After about three hours of shut-eye, I was now making the 0700-hour rounds of sick calls with the other medics, moving up and down the trenches and bunkers. Our platoon runner came by with a message from the Lieutenant informing me I was going on a daytime mission with another company. One of their medics had his arm grazed by a bullet two days ago on a patrol and had not been given a medical okay to go.

    I finished the sick calls and went to the command post bunker to give the commanding officer of our company, the Captain, the weekly platoon casualty report. The Captain, out of the blue, asked me, "Does fear ever enter your mind as a medic?" I said, "What bothers me most isn't fear, per se, it's worrying about making the right decision on what to do. A split-second decision could mean the difference of whether a man lives or dies."

    We were to take a small hill about a mile from our MLR and weed out some one hundred or more Chinese there who had been ambushing our troops heading north. After we secured the hill we would turn it over to the ROK army. We left at 1000 hours. No man's land stretched about four to six hundred yards in front of us, filled with tall grasses and willow trees. We made it through this dangerous section and reached the hill area we were looking for. The Captain called a halt while he took stock of the situation. I went about with the other medics handing out salt tablets and telling the troops to drink a lot of water. It was 98 degrees and getting hotter by the minute. With the troops wearing their heavy flak jackets, they must have felt like it was well over 100 degrees. I know I felt that way.

Looking through field glasses, the Captain could see groups of enemy huddled around small knolls. He figured the hill was probably full of Chinese hiding in gullies and bunkers. The enemy had often held their defensive positions long enough to have really dug in, making them difficult to dislodge. Rice paddies were on either side of the hill. The Captain got the four platoon leaders together to go over his plan of attack. He said, "You got your work cut out for you. Tell your troops to keep their heads and butts down."

Our platoon fanned out and took up our position around the hill. The troops were restless and ready for action. Three of our riflemen stood up and urinated on the ground. What in the hell were those guys thinking?! They were damn lucky they didn't get their asses shot off by a sniper. Things like that made my job more difficult. You learn if you want to stay alive, you never relax your guard.

Our platoon leader, a lieutenant, called for the flamethrowers to stay close to the front. We all moved forward. The hill had a thick growth of trees and shrubs for us—as well as the enemy—to hide behind. One of our squad leaders near the lead spotted a Chinese coming out of a hole on the side of the hill and shot him dead. The body was quickly seized by the feet and dragged back in. Two other caves were about twenty-five to fifty yards from that one. As we moved closer, we were met by a flurry of automatic weapons fire and the launching of hand grenades. We took cover fast. Bullets flew everywhere. I went behind a small knoll to avoid the rolling grenades coming down. The air was full of shrapnel. One of our riflemen up the hill yelled, "Doc, I'm hit!"

"Hang in there, I'm on my way!" I crawled on my belly, staying low under the bullets and shrapnel whizzing overhead. Lucky for both of us, the rifleman was behind a large tree stump, leaning against it.

Bullets pinged off the stump as I worked. The trooper had been hit in the arm and leg. Once I got the bleeding stopped, I checked for broken bones and found none. By now, the litter-bearers had made their way up to us. They had no stretcher, so the two of them would have to help him crawl down the hill little by little, staying low to the ground. It would be no easy task. The terrain was a bitch.

It was a sizzling 100 degrees by 1530 hours (3:30 p.m.). So far our troops were hanging in there. Our flamethrowers worked their slaughter, going into action from cave to cave. The blasts of fire were no doubt the most terrifying sounds the enemy heard. Hand-to-hand fighting broke out whenever the Chinese darted from one small knoll to another. Bayonets and knives flashed. After each round of hand-to-hand combat, I'd have my share of badly gashed bodies to bandage. Many of the wounds were so deep the men needed blood plasma and further treatment. Our four personnel carriers and six litter jeeps filled up fast.

We had our sights on the top of the hill, about fifty yards up. We had driven the enemy out of their holes, caves, and all other places of concealment in one final burst of teeth-grinding fury. Our BARs and machine guns blasted their way to the hilltop, killing the last few enemy left. As we worked our way toward the top, we passed dead Chinese, sometimes so many we had to tread on them. Once the bunkers were empty of enemy, the entrances were hosed with the flamethrowers and then blown shut with demolitions. Our platoon joined up with the other three at the summit and began to help with the mop up. During a mop up, we look around to see if any of the enemy are still alive, either wounded or playing dead. We found none that day.

It was now 1830 hours (6:30 p.m.). We medics headed down the hill to care for more of our wounded. In our company, nine heroes were dead and thirty-three were badly wounded. With their help, our mission had been accomplished. Our platoon was battered and our company was a mess, but still intact. I did survive—how, I do not know. A few bullets had grazed my helmet and my flak jacket looked like someone had taken pot shots at it. It had been an unbelievable ordeal.

CHAPTER 24

GREENHORNS NO MORE

This would be the first contact with the enemy for our greenhorns. We left our MLR on a mission to secure three hills that were lost two weeks ago. Once we could secure them, an ROK regiment would take them over. Our battalion leader was a gold leaf—a major, and a veteran of World War II. He'd been around the block a few times. Our company's new replacements were eager for combat.

By our third day out, we had taken the two smaller hills with light casualties. One of the dead was our radioman. He was a great guy and he died doing a helluva job. We needed to secure the big hill now, to use as a jump-off point for our push to the north later. The Chinese had a garrison of some one thousand men defending it.

At 0700 hours, the temperature was 90 degrees already and we were en route to the hill about an hour away. I and the other medics were still looking after the walking wounded from our last engagement. Most had shrapnel wounds to the legs, arms, or backsides. Their flak jackets had saved them from sure death. We brought our wounded along in weapons carriers for the trip, so I was riding in a weapons carrier pulling out shrapnel with a pair of tweezers—a slow process. We medics gave out salt tablets to counter the sweat lost in the hot, humid weather. We also passed out quinine tablets for treating malaria. The pills worked for one day only. If the men missed a day, they could catch malaria from the hordes of mosquitos. We'd joke that the mosquitos were so big they could carry away your cup of coffee. Some troops got malaria even when taking the pills—I did, and I never missed a day taking them. I didn't get it too bad, though, and just kept working when I got the fevers.

As we got close to our target, the Major sent out a platoon-size scouting party. They radioed back that the terrain ahead was rocky, wooded, and gullied with swift-running streams. They had run into intense small arms fire and mortar fire. The hill was well fortified with all sizes of bunkers. Our best bet was to send the big guns up to a ridge of our hill, facing the target hill, which was not a hill but a mountain even higher than the one we were on.

When the Chinese spotted us, they greeted us with a barrage of mortar fire and automatic weapons fire. This was going to be a long day at the office. Orders were that one company would climb up the left side of the hill while another worked their way up the right side. Our company would lead the main body up the front, and the fourth company would stay in reserve to aid any of the others. First, we had to fight our way to the base of the hill. Our big howitzers and big mortars banged away for an hour, shifting fire as directed by our well-placed observers watching for the enemy's artillery and machine guns. The earth shook, and our ears ached from the noise. Big trees splintered like matchsticks and great holes were gouged into the ground. The mid-day heat hit 102 degrees. We made it two hundred yards forward, but not without casualties. So far the battalion had fourteen dead and thirty-five wounded. In another hour and a half of hellish fighting, we crawled the last two hundred yards.

As we reached the base of the hill, the Chinese threw grenades. All three of our companies assaulted the hill, firing against a hail of burp gun fire and mortars and engaging in hand-to-hand combat. Our howitzers and mortars fired over us to the top of the hill, hitting the Chinese garrison hard. Our company was pinned down by fierce fire from a big bunker above us. Some of the men from my platoon crawled to a knoll about twenty-five yards from the bunker, and one of our squad leaders went blazing away with his BAR, covering for our two flamethrowers to move up. They fired napalm into the bunker, and Chinese ran out screaming and covered in flames. They were quickly gunned down.

Our squad leader was hit by sniper fire. With two riflemen covering, I crawled into the culvert where he was lying. I cleaned up the blood, bandaged him, and put his arm in a sling. Our litter-bearers showed up and told us our company was taking a hell of a beating and casualties were high. I had them come with me and two riflemen, moving farther up the hill. Our squad leader could work his way down the hill by himself to our makeshift aid station.

Our platoon lost five more men to sniper fire. We covered them up and left them to be picked up later. We still had a ways to go before getting to the top of the hill. Huge mortar holes were everywhere, and hundreds of Chinese bodies covered the ground, more dropping all over the place. Our machine gunners blasted away. I will never forget the experience of crawling over all those still-warm dead Chinese bodies to get to our wounded.

Our troops were now using their .75mm recoilless rifles to fire white phosphorus shells at the enemy bunkers. The Major called for an air strike and we got help from two Corsairs. They flew in, plastering the Chinese position with napalm bombs. Napalm jelly ran down the side of the hill as the whole top of the hill burst into flames—toasted. How could anyone live through that? Napalm sticks to everything so you can't get it off, you just burn up like a white hot torch.

As we moved further up the hill, we came across Chinese soldiers lying in a zombie-like state, looking stunned and dazed with their eyes open. They were dead, probably from the burning napalm sucking all the oxygen out of the air and leaving carbon monoxide. When we reached the top of the hill, I was shocked to see hundreds more dead Chinese. They had been massacred by our big mortars and artillery, then by napalm. Burnt arms, legs, heads, torsos strewn everywhere. We searched through all the mess of that hill to pick up any of our wounded and dead. When we finished, I told the other medics, "You can't just pick out one or two heroes. Every man on that hill was a hero." Our new replacements were greenhorns no more.

CHAPTER 25

HAUNTING EYES

This was the third time in six days that our company had taken this hill. My platoon had lost eighteen men. Our other three platoons had been hit just as bad or worse. The other companies in our battalion had been fighting their butts off on three other hills to the left and right of us. The last battle for our hill could only be described as a nightmare in hell. At times it had been an all-out slugfest of hand-to-hand combat with the tenacious North Korean soldiers. It was not like them to battle day in and day out for a hill, but for some reason these four small hills were of importance to them.

We had battled for some eleven hours nonstop, then a stillness had set in at midnight. We took advantage of the lull. I ran back to our medical bunker to refill my aid kits and get more tags. I had run out of the tags with so many casualties, both wounded and killed. I was hoping to get some shut-eye, too. I hadn't slept much in these six days, only a catnap here and there. The other medics in our company were in the same boat. But, that's the life of a combat medic—go, go, go, day and night, patching up and checking on our troopers and keeping up our supplies.

Lucky for us it was a mild week of late summer weather, around 85 degrees in the day and 55 at night. I followed our platoon leader, the Lieutenant, as he went up and down the trenches encouraging the men to hang in there and to hold their fire, like the old saying, *until you see the whites of their eyes*. "We don't want to run out of ammo," he told them, "Even though we're under strength, we have to hold the hill until help arrives." The LT was no 90-day wonder, one of those guys who came out of ninety days of Office Candidate School thinking he knew everything. He had earned his rank through experience.

At 0500 hours a barrage of mortar shells—incoming mail, like a calling card—turned the pre-dawn darkness into artificial daylight. Here they come again, the valley floor nothing but a mass of North Korean troops. Intelligence reports had estimated a force of some 50,000 or more would hit our sector of the MLR. A force of some 100,000 hit us earlier in the week. Nothing but bodies over bodies. It seemed that when our troops shot one, five more replaced him.

Mortar round after mortar round landed around us. The shelling lasted for some ten minutes. The idea was to soften us up for their big push up the hill, and they were doing a good job of it. When the shelling stopped, I heard, "Down here, Doc, Position 2!"

Position 2 was one of our six machine gun emplacements. I found the gunner slumped over his gun. I told his assistant to take over. The gunner was in a lot of pain and things didn't look good. I strapped his arms over my shoulders and carried him along in the trench as incoming mail landed above us. I got him to a bunker fifty feet away, and as I kicked open the door, I saw a buddy medic had just finished working on a leg wound on one of our riflemen. We put the gunner on a bunk and took off his bulletproof vest. He was in mild shock. A large piece of shrapnel had torn through the back of his right shoulder. Good thing he had on that vest. We laid him on his stomach. My buddy medic gave him a shot of morphine while I started work on his shoulder.

First I had to pull that big piece of shrapnel out. Using scissors, I cut open the back of his jacket and t-shirt. With a small knife, I cut the shrapnel out. I cleaned the wound with hydrogen peroxide, stuffed it with gauze, put on battle dressings, and put his arm in a sling. Litter-bearers would take him down first as he was the more serious of the two wounded. I headed out to more cries for help.

Making my way along the winding trenches, I found more of our troops torn up. Dead bodies lay everywhere. Our litter-bearers ran up and down the trenches picking up our dead and wounded as fast as they could. Bullets zinged over our heads and mortars threw dirt into the trenches. I came upon one of our riflemen with his stomach completely blown away by a mortar blast. I tagged him KIA.

In the midst of the raging battle, one of the North Koreans crawled up to our trench line. He stood up to thrust his bayonet at our squad leader, but our squad leader saw him, parried the thrust, then stabbed the enemy with a dagger knife, killing him. An incoming mortar round landed, knocking out one of our machine gun emplacements. The gunner and two others were blown ten feet through the air, their bodies agonizing, pitted masses of shrapnel wounds, some of the worst cases I had ever seen.

I yelled, "Code Red Position 4!" The three troopers had shrapnel in every inch of their bodies not covered by their bulletproof vests. Faces, arms, legs, blood everywhere. Almost nothing was left of their fatigues. I worked at removing pieces of shrapnel one by one. Help arrived—my buddy medic and four litter-bearers—but too late. The men died looking up at the sun just coming through the clouds.

I worked my way back to Position 2. Spent cartridge shells cluttered the area. The assistant machine gunner was going at it big time. In front of him was a pile of dead North Korean bodies. His gun was getting too hot. He continued to trigger-burst until the barrel began steaming, then kicked the gun up over the trench and down the hill, grabbed another machine gun, set it up, and continued to fire. We had been going at it now for some four and a half hours. The fire from both sides was murderous. The enemy was still coming, getting shot or blown up and killed by the hundreds. Our side had a lot of heroes, most of them now dead.

To get to us, the enemy had to crawl up, like we did when taking the hill earlier. They had to climb forbidding cliffs and ridges and over terrain as wild and inhospitable as any in all Korea. The

Lieutenant thought it would be a good time to give the enemy some of their own medicine—mortars. Within minutes our big mortars were landing in the valley below. That went on for the next ninety minutes. Then the insanity started again. Gunfire and the human wave attacks. Our machine gunners fired until their barrels glowed red and sagged from the heat. The men would then set up another gun and continue to fire. The North Koreans sent their own calling cards, more mortars, but this time they added artillery, placing solid-shot and explosive shells all along our MLR. Men went sailing into the air, others were simply torn apart.

I was in Position 5 when I heard "Doc, Doc, Position 3!" I rushed over to help in my buddy medic's area. The squad leader said three of his troops had gone topside to get more ammo when an artillery round hit. My buddy medic went up to give aid, but another round landed, hitting him, too. "Call the litter-bearers, fast!" I told him and then went topside to assess the damage. One of the three was a corporal. His arm and leg had been blown off. I could not save him. I crawled over to the other two troopers. "Hang in there, I'll be back soon."

I crawled over to reach our medic. He was the most seriously hurt. One of the litter-bearers ran back to our medical bunker for units of plasma. After working on our medic's wounds, I had the litter-bearer watch over the plasma so I could take care of the other men. In times like this, if I didn't have a litter-bearer around, I would have stuck the bayonet of a gun into the ground and hung the plasma bag on the gun stock.

The other litter-bearer was putting field dressings on the other two wounded. I took care of one trooper's face wounds, then told the litter-bearers, "Super job! Now take these men down to the aid station before more rounds come in."

I headed back toward my Position 1 area. Running up the trench toward me was one of our sergeants and two riflemen. The riflemen would be my protection—an enemy soldier had gotten through our MLR line of coiled barbed wire and hit one of our troopers. With a rifleman in front of me and one behind, I headed for our wounded man. He had rolled down about twenty feet from our trench line and lay out in the open. I said, "I have to get our guy or he'll die."

"You're crazy, you'll never make it!"

"It's my job to try." They wished me luck. On the count of three, I crawled up and over our trench line. With the riflemen covering me, I crawled about ten feet. I yelled to the wounded, "Stay where you are, don't move!" I started forward again but ducked when a burst of burp gun bullets sprayed us. As soon as that strip was laid down, I ran for cover behind a tree stump. I saw the enemy aiming for our wounded. As I ran forward, the enemy stood up and was about to put my lights out when our two riflemen opened up, killing him instantly.

Our wounded was lying in a pool of his own blood. His body was riddled up and down and he knew he was dying. "Will you pray for me, Doc?" As I put my hand on his shoulder and started my prayer, his eyes looked deep into mine and then he went limp. I paused a moment, but then another round of mortars came rumbling through our sector so I quickly tagged the trooper, put one dog tag between his teeth and the other in my aid kit with the other nine from our platoon, and ran for our trench line. I hugged the two riflemen who had saved me from certain death and told them thanks. As they took off down the trench, I looked skyward and said, "Thanks again for watching over me."

Enemy mortar rounds were still zooming all around, many of them falling short and killing their own troops. I was dead tired. I took a drink of water out of my canteen, then took a couple of deep breaths. *Okay body, let's go. There's a war going on.* Hand grenades came hurling up toward our trench lines as the gooks began a last ditch charge to take the hill they so badly wanted. Our rifle and machine gun fire crisscrossed with deadly results, but some of the enemy reached our trench line. Bayonets and hand-to-hand combat ensued. The battle lasted for some two more hours, then the enemy mortar and artillery fire stopped and the soldiers retreated.

The Lieutenant rallied a group of men for a final assault against the surviving enemy. The hill was under our control. Our flag went up. Flags went up on the other three hills. By 1815 hours (6:15 p.m.), we finished mopping up the area. The litter-bearers took all our dead heroes down the backside of the hill to go to Graves Registration. As the bodies were put on the litter jeeps, the chaplain said, "All are called upon to take that journey to no return." I could only say, "R.I.P." I couldn't forget the haunting eyes of the young soldier as I prayed for him.

CHAPTER 26

OUTPOST NO MORE

The most dreaded duty on the front line was that of the outpost. The men there were to give advance warning only, not to defend anything. The Chinese and North Koreans were constantly probing us, pulling raids and attacks. When the enemy fired their artillery and mortar rounds, the one place on earth you did not want to be was on your own at an outpost.

Outpost positions sat forward of the MLR and varied in distance away, mostly from fifty to five hundred yards, but some much further. Usually the men were protected with bunkers or sandbag walls. After dusk, the outpost became a checkpoint for troops going out on night patrols, raids, and ambushes. An outpost often consisted of fewer than twelve men, but in some cases up to a platoon or more. The time spent there varied from one night to a week, in some cases a month or longer. Night duty was long and eerie. The company CO usually rotated this dangerous duty so that each man in the company had a turn at it.

This early fall morning was a muggy 90 degrees. Our sector along the MLR was relatively quiet as it had been for the last two days. This allowed our front line troops and the men on outpost duty to take a breather. Our company's MLR frontage was approximately two miles long, and our outpost was 150 yards forward. After I gave medical clearance to seven men in our platoon, they crossed over the wire and crawled under the cover of early morning darkness down the forward slope to start their 0600 shift. They would be relieved from their duties after twelve hours.

For most of the day, I checked on our troops and worked back in our medical aid bunker some forty to fifty yards behind our MLR, on the protected back slope of our hill. Our aid bunker had a desk made by laying a board across stacked ammo boxes that served as legs. As the sun went down behind the high mountains, I made it up the trench to watch the outpost relief team cross the wire. I wished them good luck. Our outpost, using the sound power phone, called our platoon leader, a lieutenant, to say they were taking small arms fire and shutting the door to the bunker.

Suddenly, mortar rounds slammed the outpost area like a hailstorm. Our sector went on red alert. The siren went off and medics and litter-bearers ran to their assigned areas. I was already in mine, Area 2. The outpost relief team backtracked to rejoin their platoon. We had two BAR men, one radioman, two machine gunners, and two assistants pulling duty at the outpost, all from my squad.

Along with the barrage of mortars, we now heard automatic weapons fire. Sarge, our squad leader, yelled, "Our guys are in a heap of trouble!" The LT had to use his radio to check on the men because the shelling had torn up our wires to the sound power phone. Our radioman out there was to call back from time to time to let him know what the hell was going on. LT called our mortar units asking for a few flares. In no time up went two white flares so we could see who and what size force had hit. The outpost radioed back that they were being attacked by an overwhelming number of Chinese, a battalion or more.

The initial attack was fast and furious. There was nothing we could do about it for now. The outpost team was completely on their own. If a full Chinese battalion of four companies—that's about 1,000 men—attacked our one company of some 260 men, we were in for a long firefight.

Many of the attackers were now bypassing the outpost and heading up toward our MLR. LT radioed to the mortar units, giving them the readings of enemy locations on our forward slopes. Two flares blasted high above our hill, their parachutes opened, and the flares drifted slowly down, lighting up the area in front of our lines and giving our troops some great targets to shoot at. Things were hot and heavy. I heard, "Help, Doc!" through the deafening noise. I made my way down the dark trench and found one of our troopers bent over beside his weapons position. His buddy had taken over and was firing away. I told him to keep at it. It was so dark I could not immediately see where the trooper had been hit. I laid him down in the trench and got out my penlight. When I took his helmet off, I saw blood everywhere. It appeared a main artery in his neck was nicked. His buddy yelled down, "Doc, is he going to die?"

"I'm going to do my damnedest to see that he doesn't!" I stuffed a roll of gauze under a large battle dressing and taped it up to the wound to try to stop the bleeding. The litter-bearers arrived. I tried to console the soldier—I knew he was dying. In a few short minutes it was over. His buddy looked down at me. I said, "I tried to save him." He said, "Thanks, Doc," and went back to blasting away at the oncoming enemy.

I made my way toward another cry. The trench had collapsed under the mortar shelling. I crawled in the dark, up and over the pile of dirt. Bullets and mortars flew in every direction. Keeping my body low, I finally reached the trooper calling me, but it was for his buddy. He said, "Look somewhere over there by that pile of dirt." I never found enough of the man to say that was him. I had one dog tag. When I crawled back over to the trooper, he asked if I would take a look at his arm. Another trooper came over to cover for us. I took out my penlight and used scissors to cut open the man's shirt. With tweezers I pulled out two pieces of shrapnel, then cleaned and bandaged his arm. I gave him two aspirins. With that he went back to his position and started firing away again.

Other trench areas were collapsing under all the mortar fire.

Scores of our troops lay wounded or dead. With many of our dead, we medics could only ID them by their dog tags. LT went around telling our line troops to wait until the enemy was about thirty meters away and then fire. He called the outpost to ask how things were going. They replied their bunker was still under attack. The rest of our platoon at the MLR bore the brunt of the enemy's attack and concentrated fire. After hours of fighting, we were still taking a severe beating. "Doc, Doc, up here!" Staying low in the trench with bullets whizzing by like mosquitoes, I headed toward the cry for help.

I found the trooper lying in the trench. He had taken bullets to both legs. I put a tourniquet high on each thigh, then pulled him up across my shoulder in a fireman's carry. With a rifleman in front and another behind, I made my way to the ammo bunker about twenty or so yards away. The riflemen used my penlight to find some rifles to use as leg splints. They came back with four carbines, better because they were slimmer and lighter than the Garand rifles. I gave the trooper a shot of morphine and the litter guys at the bunker took care of splinting while I wrote up the tag. I was so damned exhausted! The trooper was taller and heavier than me. Where I got the strength to carry him, I don't know. The litter-bearers took him down our back slope under a hail of bullets. As I left the bunker, screams for "Doc!" came from all around.

It was pitch black out and to make things worse the trenches were piling up with Chinese bodies. The stench of death and the smell of blood was everywhere. We medics had a hard time finding our downed men and telling who was dead and who was wounded. Sarge came running up saying the LT told him to stay close to me, just in case. I was glad to have him along for my protection.

I think the Chinese saw that our company was not a pushover and that they had a fight on their hands, but they kept picking away looking for any weakness. We heard one helluva blast up the trench lines and Sarge and I took off toward the noise. The trench was no more. We crawled around, using my penlight to assess damages and determine who needed treatment first. Bodies of wounded and dead lay mixed in the pile of rubble. I reminded myself to stay composed. Sarge went off to find riflemen to provide cover for us. I went about seeing to the wounded. Who was hurt the worst? A trooper yelled, "Doc, I just have shrapnel wounds. Take care of my buddy first. He's on that pile of dirt."

Litter-bearers arrived to help. Sarge came back with riflemen to provide cover as he and I went to look for the other wounded. Leaning up against the dirt was a trooper holding his belly. On closer look, we saw he was holding some of his intestines. I gave the trooper a shot of morphine and carefully folded his intestines up and put them back into his body. That's a slow process. In bad cases, I had to stack the small intestines first, then the large intestines, dirt and all. They would stick to my hands. I'd zigzag stitch the wound to roughly close it, no anesthetic but the morphine shot. No time for stitching now. I went back to see to the guy's buddy after calling for a couple litter-bearers to help Sarge wrap dressings around the trooper's belly to hold things in place.

I found the litter-bearers had done a super job of patching up the other guy. With mortar rounds still coming in and the sound of automatic weapons fire above, all of us worked to put the two wounded on stretchers. With the help of the riflemen and with Sarge leading the way, the litter-bearers took the men down our back slopes to the battalion aid station.

On my way back down the trench to Area 2, a mortar round landed just twenty yards in front of our MLR. I lay dazed, flat on my face in the trench. My helmet was some fifteen feet away. When I picked it up, I found one side had a jagged crease where a piece of shrapnel had run and then dug a dent as big as a walnut. When Sarge caught up with me, I showed him my helmet. "The gods are on your side!" he said.

Communications to the company outpost was bad due to the incoming mortars and general confusion, but the enemy had been noticeably less active in the last hour or so. As Sarge and I worked our way back to the aid bunker so I could load up on more supplies, one of our line troopers came running by yelling the Chinese were withdrawing back down into the valley. Sarge said, "LT had it right. They must have run out of ammo and manpower."

It took us medics and litter-bearers four hours to tend to our wounded and prepare for the next assault, which was certain to come. At dawn the LT, with a squad of men along with us medics and litter-bearers, headed down to the outpost. I said, "Nobody could have survived that pounding!" As we got closer, we saw the outpost bunker had been completely pulverized. It was no more. Someone famous once said something to the effect that each time a man dies, the rest of us, too, die a little bit.

"No man is an island… any man's death diminishes me, because I am involved in mankind, and therefore never send to know for whom the bell tolls; it tolls for thee." –John Donne

CHAPTER 27

NAPALM BURNING

Our battalion had left in the wee hours of the morning on a special mission. We conducted a search and destroy operation through two villages, looking for suspected North Korean forces that Intelligence said might be hiding there. We found none. The villages we came across were usually a bunch of huts made of straw, but sometimes they had some wooden structures with straw roofs. The people were poor and had very little. The Korean military took over everything, even the crops they tried to grow. We'd tell the Mama-sans and Papa-sans they'd be okay, that we weren't going to hurt them, then we'd look for enemy soldiers. A lot of times the villagers told us where the North Korean troops had gone. Sometimes we'd leave a couple squads with the villagers to be on guard, keeping our rear escape open for when we returned back that way.

The Mama-sans in these villages carried loads of kids strapped to them. They cooked something they called *gohan* in big black kettles. This was a watery soup with vegetables and lots of garlic. The people smelled like garlic. Sometimes we'd eat some of their food, whatever it was. They also ate snakes, dogs, some kind of foxlike animal, a pigeon-type bird, deer, and horse. The horsemeat was pretty tough.

At 1400 hours we headed back to home base. The temperature was a very nice 84 degrees. We were only thirty minutes away from our MLR when from on top of a hill a huge enemy force opened up on us with everything they had—machine guns, burp guns, rifles, and mortar fire. Our soldiers dropped like flies. Bullets grazed my bulletproof vest. Our company took cover in a rice paddy near the base of a hill to our right. "Doc, Doc, I'm hit!" came from every direction. Our battalion returned fire. The noise from our automatic weapons was so loud you couldn't hear the person next to you. In the seconds between volleys I listened for cries of the wounded. We medics needed to get to a small hollow about twenty-five yards away to work on our wounded in some protection. Our big mortars blasted away at the enemy hill and we all took off running zigzag. About ten feet from the hollow, one of our medics got hit. We dragged him in. He was shot in the arm and leg, but after we bandaged and taped him up, he helped us get our wounded troopers into the hollow. By now our company had nine dead and twenty-seven wounded.

Our mortars hit the enemy hard for over an hour. Our battalion commander decided it was time to call for air power. A wave of Corsair fighter planes came dropping high explosives. They didn't miss any part of that hill. Ten minutes later, a second wave dropped napalm bombs. In their foxholes, trenches, and bunkers, the enemy might have felt safe from the shelling, but staying in them now meant they would be burned alive by the intense heat of flaming napalm or suffocated from lack of oxygen. As flames closed in, many enemy left for higher ground only to be met by shrapnel from our mortar rounds and by our automatic weapons fire from below.

I was working on a soldier hit by small arms fire when a mortar round landed some twenty yards away. The blast threw me up and backward, and I fell hard to the ground. When I came around, I found small holes all through my sleeves. I pulled my sleeves up to see blood running down both arms. As I wiped it away with alcohol pads, I realized the bee stings I felt were little pieces of shrapnel embedded in my skin. They had ripped the hell out of my bulletproof vest and helmet cover. When I got back to home base I would have to pick out the shrapnel with my small tweezers, but for now I just put on some battle ointment and bandaged both arms. I looked over at the soldier I had been tending, but he was dead. He must have taken the brunt of the shrapnel.

Our battalion fought tenaciously and our soldiers worked their way to the base of the enemy hill. We would assault the hill at 1800 hours (6:00 p.m.), in about fifteen minutes. From the get-go, no one really knew how big of a force we were up against. We were about to find out. But, after the beating they took from our air attack, things looked grim for them.

Our big mortars blasted away at the hill. That was our company's cue to move up our side of the hill. Our platoon leader, the Lieutenant, brought our flamethrower guys up front to finish off what was left of the enemy bunkers. As we made our way up the hill, bullets flew in front of us in a steady spray. They were coming from one bunker. Our flamethrower men crawled up to a point where they could fire long streams of burning napalm into the bunker. That took care of it, and in a few minutes four more bunkers were destroyed. The napalm and strafing from the Corsairs had made a difference, but we still had a few snipers firing down at us.

The foxholes, trenches, and bunkers held hundreds of burnt bodies and were still hot from the napalm of a few hours ago. The North Korean troops were in shambles. We swarmed up and over the slopes of the hill. The enemy made a brave attempt to hold on. Instead of giving ground, they contested every inch and looked to be holding their position to the last man. When the end was near, though, a number of them scurried down the back of the hill only to be met by our automatic weapons fire.

Once we had firmly fastened the stretcher for the last of our most wounded soldiers onto the ski skids of our hovering medevac chopper, I hooked myself on the outside of the chopper to administer blood plasma to our trooper. I tapped three times on the chopper's bubble dome cover to signal everything was a go and the chopper took off for the fifteen-minute ride back to our battalion aid station. I told the surgeon there that everyone on that hill deserved a medal. I saluted our wounded men and told them I was proud to have been their combat medic.

CHAPTER 28

EAGLE ONE

Something was in the wind. The higher ups knew that just a few hours away the North Koreans had a huge ammunition depot and a motor depot that housed trucks and weapons carriers. Maybe we could beat them to the punch by pulling off a raid to put those out of commission. A fifteen-man team was selected for a two-day mission behind enemy lines. I was asked to go as the medic. We'd be on a patrol to weed out insurgents who had been probing our sector for the last few days. That was our cover.

We met in the company command post. Our leader was not just any colonel, but a commando we were to call Eagle One. He knew how to move at night and he had eagle eyes—could see anything that moved or climbed or crawled. I had gone with him on a previous mission. He was good—damn good. We were paired into eight teams. The radioman and I were Team 8. Aerial reconnaissance confirmed the locations of the munitions depot and motor depot near remote and sparsely populated villages. We would destroy the munitions depot first, then the motor depot on our way home. We each got a tote bag to bring along. We were not to open them until told.

The team met at our MLR, our faces and hands blackened. The sun was low over the hills. Eagle One himself checked each man: dog tags taped together, dagger in shield, compass, canteen full of water, bulletproof vest. The men were loaded with enough explosives to blow up a small town or two. I had both aid kits full up, plus an extra medical shoulder bag—in case things got a little dicey. My web belt held a holstered .45 with silencer. When we reached the valley below our hill we opened our tote bags. Inside each was a North Korean officer or non-commissioned officer uniform. I put on a senior lieutenant uniform. Eagle One wore a colonel's. We put on Korean-style tennis shoes, then taped down the bottoms of our pants legs. Team 1 dug a large hole and buried our U.S. uniforms.

We moved through no man's land. Darkness was approaching. As we neared the enemy's hill, two point men went to scout ahead. They found a wide area between hills where the enemy wasn't patrolling. We went single file, five feet apart, through that gap. It was a perfect night for a raid—cloudy with no moonlight, which also made it damned difficult to see anything more than a few feet ahead.

We moved north through a dense, jungle-like forest, then we began a torturous climb over a steep, rocky ridge. I told Eagle One we needed to stop for medical care, just ten minutes. "Okay, Doc, no longer." One man had a gash on his thigh from a sharp rock. I cut open his uniform to see the wound, using my penlight with a team member hiding the light from any enemy eyes. When I finished taking care of it, brown tape worked to hold together the cut pants leg, blending in with the brown security officer uniform. I finished with forty seconds to spare. Eagle One said, "That's why we picked you, Doc."

We climbed over the ridge and down into a valley. We were ten minutes through the valley when one of our point men came running back. A small group of soldiers was coming our way. We got down behind a low mound. When the enemy was within ten feet of us, our point men gave a quick burst of their burp guns. Eight North Koreans lay dead. We covered their bodies with thick foliage and moved on.

We arrived at our first objective. A few dim lights shone in the village. With Eagle One leading, we made our way around the village to a large rice paddy and leapfrogged through the damp dirt to within twenty-five yards of the depot. "Set your watches. We have an hour and a half to pull off this caper."

We crept toward the depot. Timing was everything. Teams 1 and 2 were to eliminate the guards at the four observation towers. Under cover of darkness, they crawled to within ten feet of each tower and took aim, silencers on. At precisely the same moment, the four guards—shot in the head—fell dead over the railings and onto the ground below. From intelligence reports, their replacements would arrive for duty at midnight.

Eagle One, the radioman, and the interpreter remained behind to cover our exit. I stayed with them. Our little group had firepower. We each carried .45 caliber pistols and the radioman and the interpreter also had carbines with five 15-round clips, plus they carried grenades. Eagle One had a burp gun and grenades. Teams 3, 4, 5, and 6 left to fasten detonation caps on their plastic explosives and blocks of TNT and tape them onto the barbed-wire fence posts set around the depot. Teams 1 and 2 would cover them. The timers would be set to go off thirty minutes after the job was done, giving us time to get far enough away. As my group waited, the others finished and popped up out of the darkness, right on time.

We made our way around the village and scrambled up the path toward the top of the hill to our rendezvous point. Eagle One told us, "Get your asses as low as you can behind the trees!" On time, the whole munitions depot went sky high. The noise was deafening. Flames shot up, debris flying everywhere. Eagle One thought maybe any enemy left alive would think the explosion was an accident. I figured everyone in or near the village was probably dead. I thought about the civilians that might have been there, but I also remembered what Eagle One had said in our briefing. "Commando missions are dirty, ugly, and nasty."

Eagle One led us through the rugged terrain and blackness of the forest. We could see only about ten feet in front of us. Soon we were out of range of the noises from the explosions. A small stream was just ahead. Eagle One asked if I had any Halazone tablets. I did. He motioned the men to come one at a time to fill their canteens. As they did, I gave each a tablet to purify their water for drinking.

We made it through the most rugged part of the forest, an exhausting climb. Every few yards seemed to be steeper and rockier than the last, and in many places our path was narrow and winding. Heading down into a valley, we stopped on a mound overlooking the depot compound. Our two point men found the village was mostly simple straw huts. All was quiet. The motor depot compound had a large work shed. In front of the shed, fenced in on three sides with barbed wire, was a huge lot with about fifty or more military trucks and other vehicles. The depot had only one guard. A small light shone at the shed entrance and another at the gate entrance.

Our teams had one hour to set their charges. A Team 1 man, the radioman, and I would cover our exit. Team 2 would do away with the gate guard and our Korean interpreter would replace him. Our tennis shoes let us move quietly without being heard. We crept our way to a nearby mound overlooking our target. My group could now observe what would go on. I knew what would happen next.

As Eagle One, dressed as a North Korean colonel, walked toward the motor depot gate, he motioned to our interpreter, dressed as a North Korean corporal, to switch position with the gate guard. The guard walked toward Eagle One, stopped, and saluted him. Eagle One raised his .45 caliber weapon with silencer and fired two shots, killing the guard instantly. He dragged the body off into a small ditch a few feet away. Our men cut the gate's lock and went inside, laying their charges within row after row of trucks and other vehicles.

As the men were finishing up, our Team 1 man motioned that he had heard a suspicious noise and was going down to alert the others. As he took off, we, too, heard noises, and not far away. The radioman had his weapon set up on the top of our mound. He motioned for me to stay low. Suddenly our Team 1 man came running toward us, loudly whispering our password. Right behind him was Eagle One leading all the others. "Move out!"

Making our way around the mound, we were greeted by small arms fire. As we raced past a big rice paddy and the village, Eagle One yelled, "Count to ten and hit the ditch!" Just as we hit the ground, the whole motor depot blasted sky high. "Now let's get the hell out of here!" Right behind us were the North Koreans, firing with everything they had. Our men turned and blasted away. The fighting was brief, and when it was over nine gooks lay dead. Four of our men had been hit. We had to stop so I could see the severity of their wounds. We ducked into dense bushes. The other team members set up a perimeter around me so I could go to work. Eagle One said, "Let's go, Doc, we don't have all day."

Two of the men had only been grazed by bullets, but one man had an arm wound and another had a hand wound with broken bones. I taped a small splint to the hand then wrapped it as best I could with two battle dressings. The man looked like he had on a boxing glove. I put his arm in a sling and gave him a shot of morphine. Eagle One asked, "Doc, can they fire their weapons?" I said if they needed to they could shoot, but I warned that two of them would have a helluva time climbing the rugged hills using only their right arms.

Eagle One and our Korean interpreter took the point. We were about three quarters of the way down a hill when our interpreter smelled garlic. He could smell the strong odor of other Koreans from some five hundred yards away. He was damn good at it. On other missions he had saved our butts by scenting the enemy. Eagle One and the interpreter took off down the trail and found a group of enemy soldiers, a patrol of some kind. They were heading for the same valley we were.

It was daylight now, a cloudy morning of about 50 to 60 degrees. We were about eight hundred yards from our rendezvous area. We had to beat the enemy down into the valley. With our injured trailing, we made it down the hill not knowing if the enemy had, too. Now we had to cross the valley floor. We took off running double time, my aid kits hitting my ass every step of the way. We ran into a big rice paddy. On the other side were small trees and bushes where we could take cover. As we started to cross the damp paddy, small arms and automatic weapons fire came at us from the bottom of the hill. We hit the ground, pinned down out in the open. Lucky for us, the gook patrol was far enough away or we all would have been dead meat.

Eagle One took out his field glasses. Enemy soldiers were strung out across the valley floor in a holding mode. Out of nowhere, a volley of mortars landed in front of our paddy field, shrapnel flying everywhere. After a few minutes of incoming mail, another hail of bullets came zipping over our heads. When it was over, I heard, "Doc, over here!"

Crawling as low as I could in between the rows of rice plants, I reached our wounded. He was lying on his side, his right arm hit by shrapnel. When I rolled him on his back, blood was everywhere. I quickly put a tourniquet as high as I could on the arm to stop the bleeding. A big piece of shrapnel was sticking out of his forearm so I got out my tweezers and pulled it out. As best I could tell, no fractures. I cleaned the wound and wrapped it. "Hold still," I said, and gave him a shot of morphine.

Eagle One yelled, "We're going to make a run for it!" We leapfrogged our way across the rice paddy toward the small trees beyond, bullets flying. I thought, *this is it for me*. But we all made it and huddled among the trees. I checked over our wounded and gave the okay. As we started to leave, a barrage of mortars came raining down on the paddy field behind us. We would have been toast there a few minutes earlier.

Under cover of the small trees, bushes, and tall grass, we moved as quickly as we could to our rendezvous area. Following along a dirt path, our Korean interpreter point man smelled a strong garlic odor again. We scattered. I paired up with our radioman, staying with him behind some trees in a low gully, about ten yards from the path. He whispered, "Keep your ass down. I'll tell you when to get up. Ass down!"

We waited and waited until even I could smell the garlic. I raised my head a bit to look between the branches of a tree. A small patrol of enemy soldiers came up the path. Eagle One let them pass right in front of us, but when they got about ten yards past us, our men blasted away. I was in the middle of a shooting gallery! Bullets flew from both sides. One almost took my helmet off. I got the message and needed no further invitation to keep my ass down. In less than ten minutes it was all over.

Eagle One hollered for his men to hold their fire and check in. When the count was over, we had four more wounded, but none dead. All twelve enemy were dead, their bodies sprawled up and down the dirt path. I set up shop behind a big stump to take care of our wounded. The rest of the men set up a perimeter around me. Eagle One said, "Doc, we've got to get the hell out of here fast!"

"Give me twenty minutes." I had two thigh wounds and two arm wounds to care for. With a little help from some of the men, we were ready to go and took off down the path for our rendezvous area. I told our radioman, "I don't think we've seen the last of the bad guys."

We reached our rendezvous area, but now had to cross some six hundred yards of no man's land. Three hundred of those were in the enemy's half. "We fight our way out!" No sooner had we begun to move when the enemy reappeared to claim their part of the territory. They raked us with burp gun and rifle fire. We ducked behind anything and everything. There were shrubs and small trees, but we were still pretty much out in the open. It was a damn good thing we had leftover ammo and charges.

Eagle One signaled for the men to hold their fire. Then out of nowhere a patrol of gooks was within fifty feet of us. On command our entire team erupted with BAR fire and grenades. Eagle One yelled, "Doc, I'm hit!" I crawled over as fast as I could. As I finished bandaging his arm, suddenly the firing stopped. Bodies littered the pathway. I had to check the enemy to make sure all were dead. Two of our men were my guards in case some of the bodies were still alive and dangerous. I counted ten dead enemy and two more of our men wounded. I told Eagle One I would have both our guys taken care of in fifteen minutes.

We moved out at a snail-like pace trying to attract as little attention as possible. Our interpreter point man got wind of more enemies—again he smelled them. He went ahead to survey the terrain. Eagle One gave the sign for his men to V out and lay low among the bushes and trees. They were to use their silencers. Again we waited. Four rag-tag North Korean soldiers came by. Once they passed through, our men picked them off as if they were at a turkey shoot.

We filed out two abreast in a fifty-foot-long column. We crossed into our side of no man's land as the sun was just starting to go down behind the high mountains. As we got near our front line, Eagle One made sure we stayed hidden so as not to be seen by our troops—we were still dressed as North Korean officers. At our rendezvous area at the bottom of our hill, Eagle One got on the radio to tell home base to pass the word to all units that we were returning from our patrol and to hold fire. Now we had to uncover our own uniforms, put them on, and bury our North Korean uniforms. As we crossed the wire of our MLR, Eagle One told us, "Job well done!"

CHAPTER 29

BEHIND ENEMY LINES

The top of the letter was stamped "Classified – Top Secret." My tired eyes opened wide. It was 0400 hours and I had just come back from a hit-and-run raid deep into enemy territory. Heading down the trench to our medical bunker, I had come across two MP, military police. They wanted to talk to me. I needed some shut-eye and asked if they'd come along with me to the bunker. Once there, I was handed an envelope. I sat on my bunk and turned up the oil lamp so I could read. I was going to a MASH unit in the rear echelon to learn about a new burn ointment. I would be part of the testing team with nine other combat medics. I was to leave in ten minutes, bringing my aid kits.

So much for sleep. I followed the MPs down the backside of our hill to a waiting jeep. We drove to a chopper pad, and there was a chopper and its pilot ready to go. Landing at the MASH pad, I met three men with no bars and no obvious rank. I got in the back of the jeep with one of them. He asked me, "Have you eaten?"

"No," I said, and told him I hadn't had any shut-eye in twenty-four hours.

"We got you covered."

We arrived at MASH, but drove past the hospital to a large tent about five hundred yards away. The place was guarded by umpteen

MPs. Inside were ten cots and one long table. One of the men asked to see my dog tags. The men and I sat down at the table. As we were about to start eating breakfast, in walked nine men. I was introduced to them. "Gentlemen, meet Doc."

After we finished eating, the man who introduced me stood up. "Let's get down to business. The only one who doesn't know the real reason why you're all here is Doc, but I think he knows it's not for a bake sale. He's done missions before and I hear he's got what it takes." During the next hour, I found out this was no burn ointment training. The meeting ended with the lead commando saying, "We're all in this together as a team, one for all, all for one. Doc, hit the sack until 1500 hours."

I was exhausted and six hours went by like six minutes. "Up and at 'em!" I heard choppers coming in. While the others checked their equipment, I checked my two aid kits and grabbed an extra surgical kit from the MASH for good measure. The men who had brought me met us at the tent entrance. As we boarded the two choppers, one of them yelled, "See you in a couple days!"

The commando leader was in the chopper with me. He handed me a clicker and told me to call him X-1. The other eight commandos were all X-2s. One click of the clicker meant forward, two clicks meant stop. X-1 told me to put on my makeup. That was the black ointment we used on our faces and on the backs of our hands. The interpreter, one of the weapons experts, and the communications radioman were in the chopper with us. In the other chopper were two demolitions experts, two snipers, and the other weapons expert.

An hour and a half later we were at our drop-off point a mile from the enemy line. Once we unloaded, our pilot wished us good luck and said he'd see us when we were done. "Just call," he said, and took off. The X-2s buried extra weapons and ammo in the dirt—we might need them in case things went bad during withdrawal.

X-1 gave the signal for everyone to get into an X formation. Our leader, the radioman, the interpreter, and I were in the middle. I thought I was in good shape, but when he said to move out fast, move out they did—in double time. It took all I had to keep up, with the two aid kits flopping up and down on my butt. To say these guys were in shape was an understatement. They were built like boulders. We made our way to a wooded area. The two snipers put on their silencers.

From the wooded area we had to go through an open section. We waited until dark. The moon disappeared behind heavy clouds. Looking through his night field glasses, X-1 scanned up and down the enemy lines. "This is it, we're going in." We crept to the edge of the woods. One sniper and one weapons expert went first. Once over the line, they would signal with one click if everything was a go. After twenty minutes, we heard the click. We would leave in groups of two or three, the last two would be X-1 and me. At the signal, the first three men left. Five minutes later, three more went, then two. Now it was our turn. We made it! Our point men left to scout ahead.

This was it, two days of hell. I remembered telling my battalion surgeon before I went on my first patrol that I was a little scared. He had replied, "You can't focus on the fear, you have to learn to control it. Fear is a good thing. It keeps you alert. Your job as a medic is to save lives, and the men are counting on you."

The signal came to move out, all clear. The first of our two objectives was three hours away. Creeping quietly in the dark was nothing new for these guys. I had a hard time keeping up. I wasn't trained to be a commando, but then they weren't trained to be medics. It would take teamwork if we were all going to get out of this alive.

A tough climb up some cliffs with the help of ropes was followed by a long and arduous climb up a steep, rocky, terraced hillside. After a few hours, we came upon a cave and hunkered down inside. The X-2s rotated guard duty. A tarp was hung over the entrance so we could use our penlights inside.

One of the X-2s said he had a cut on his arm. It was more than just a cut, he had a big gash on his forearm. I pulled open my emergency kit and got out hydrogen peroxide to clean the wound. I used multi-purpose adhesive bandages to pull the edges of skin together, then covered the area with gauze and taped up the arm with a battlefield dressing. I gave him a shot of penicillin and said, "You're ready to go."

X-1 put his map on the ground and went over every last detail of the raid with us. We dug into our C-rations while we listened. We'd be two men to a team. Team 1 was X-1 and the interpreter. Team 5 was the radioman and me. Our mission was to destroy the petrol station, the ammo depot, and the railway depot. We would make all three unusable—for the long term. The men all knew their tasks. Their expertise was in night attacks in exceptionally difficult conditions, using their initiative in disconcerting situations. I felt honored to be a part of their team.

The town was a mile or so away. We made our way slowly down the rugged hillside. Team 3 went ahead to survey the landscape. After an hour and forty-five minutes, we made it to the bottom of the hill. The radioman went to set-up his gun position to cover our withdrawal. I would be going with Team 1 now. X-1 told the men, "If anyone gets hit, don't call out 'Doc.' Call out your team number. Then Doc will know what site you're at and the enemy won't know we have a doc with us."

Team 2 left to take out the guard on the observation tower and the one in the hut below it. The rest of us waited, ready to go once we heard them click the okay. The Team 4 men were loaded with so many explosives they could have blown up the whole town. Click. "Let's go!"

Team 1 and I got to about fifty feet from the railway depot. X-1 went to survey the situation. One soldier was sitting in an armchair out in front of the station and one was at the desk inside. X-1 thought if he shot the man in the armchair, he and the chair might fall over, making a lot of noise. He told me to give the interpreter some gauze loaded with ether. When the interpreter pulled out his dagger, I understood what the plan was. Once he did away with the soldier in the chair, then X-1 would use his silencer and take out the soldier inside. Both took off into the darkness like cats on the prowl.

While waiting alone for my team to do their thing, I felt a little safer knowing that Team 2 from their position could see everything that was going on thanks to the town's dim lights. I also had my trusted .45 strapped to my shoulder, although I was no Wyatt Earp. And my team had left me a satchel full of hand grenades in case something went wrong.

Team 3 made it to the petrol station. Not a soul was around. The station had an eight-foot tall fence around it. Our men had to cut off the padlock, then lay out charges of TNT around the four storage tanks and the petrol trucks. Loaded with explosives, Team 4 had the hardest task of all. They had to knock out the ammo depot, the most important target. The ammo compound had a high fence around it as well. Two huge bunkers and four sheds held ammo for all the forward line enemy troops to use in the months to come. The team had to attach the magnetic charges and tape TNT to the bunkers and sheds and a small barracks-like building. They would set the timers to go off at 0330 hours.

I waited. At 0310 hours I clutched my satchel bag of grenades, ready to take off. I heard four clicks. I gave four clicks back. All the teams came running. "Let's get the hell out of here!"

I never ran so fast and hard in my life. When we got to the bottom of the hill, X-1 gave a signal to the radioman above. Tired and dirty, we moved swiftly to the gully in the cliff where the radioman waited. X-1 said, "Get down behind the trees. This blast will be like nothing you've ever seen." No sooner said than a huge explosion shook the ground. It was like an atomic bomb! The railway depot, the petrol station, and the ammo depot blew sky high, taking the rest of the town along. The explosions would go on for hours. I had butterflies, but all had gone well and everyone had made it. "We're on schedule, let's move-out!"

Our second target was a town just southwest of us. A bridge there crossed over a winding river that probably provided fish for food. There were only two ways into or out of the town: cross the bridge or climb over the steep hill on the backside of the town. Plans were to set charges on the bridge and blow it up at 0430 hours, then get back to our cave by 0530 hours.

We came over a hill and saw the bridge below. Team 3 went down to look things over. To their surprise no one was guarding it. We moved down the hill and the radioman set up his gun to cover the rear. Teams 3 and 4 would set up the charges, plus a row of charges to go off a half hour later to make the enemy think we were still in the area.

The teams finished and we got out of there fast. We made it back up the hill and fifty yards down the other side when the fireworks celebration went off. The terrain going back was the same nightmare, full of steep cliffs and gullies—grueling, but we made it back to the cave on time. X-1 called back to base camp. The plan was to pick us up at 2000 hours at our rendezvous area three hours away. We would wait it out for the day in the cave.

Base camp had said the enemy was patrolling up and down the lines. That included the area where we were to be picked up. X-1 would check back with base camp later. We might have to fight our way out. For now, we needed to eat our C-rations and try to get some shut-eye in that cold, dark cave.

At about 1200 hours we were up, rested, and ready to go, waiting for the call in to base camp. I checked out my aid kits and medical gear. The men checked their gear and ammo supply. X-1 was satisfied we had enough to get us out of any mess.

"Are you ready for a fight, Doc?"

"That's why I came along!"

"You're okay, Doc. I knew I could count on you."

I felt like one of them.

X-1 and the radioman went outside to contact base camp again. X-1 was not one to pull any punches. "We're fighting our way out. We leave at 1700 hours." He went over the plan, then called me over. "It could get nasty out there. Whatever happens, stick with me." I was sitting with the radioman. He said, "X-1 will get us all out of this mess." I sure hoped so.

There was a chill in the air. My thermometer read 55 degrees. We took the same way back as coming in, stopping to bury a bag of our empty C-rations trash. We didn't want to leave any trace that we had been there. I was back with our radioman and asked him about our new click signals. When it got dark, with our faces blackened and the black outfits we were wearing, sometimes it was hard to see the other teams. We heard three clicks and stopped. Four enemy soldiers were ahead taking a cigarette break. X-1 sent Teams Two and Three to do away with them by way of the dagger. In twenty minutes, mission accomplished.

We seesawed our way down to the valley below. Several paths crossed our way. X-1 pondered which one to take. I was glad for the break because I needed water, and to be honest, I was completely pooped. X-1 radioed back to home base for last minute details. Our pickup was now at 2100 hours, not 2000 hours.

We headed up the path that led due west according to X-1's compass. He gave three clicks and we dove for cover. To our right and coming up the hillside, a group of North Korean soldiers raced toward us blasting away with burp guns and throwing hand grenades. X-1 threw a flare that burst high in the sky, lighting up the hillside. Our men waited, then opened up with everything they had. Under the glare of the white flare the North Korean soldiers fell one by one. In minutes it was all over. Twenty yards away lay ten dead enemy soldiers, just a small band looking for us. X-1 yelled to his teams to check in by numbers. "Three, one hit!"

One of the Team 3 men had been hit in the arm by shrapnel. His buddy held my penlight, covering the light the best he could while I took care of the wound. The enemy had sharp eyes and could even see the light of cigarettes in the dark. With sighs of relief, we rested. In the distance we heard the sound of choppers. From the hillside, we also heard guns firing. As the two choppers hovered low, doors open, we ran like hell for them. The choppers engaged the oncoming enemy with machine gun fire. Our interpreter, running beside me, took a stray bullet to the leg. I threw his arm over my shoulder, and half carried him. X-1 and the radioman pulled him up into the chopper. I jumped in just as both choppers took off under a hail of bullets. I went to work on our interpreter's leg. Looking down at my watch, I saw we had taken off at our scheduled pickup—unbelievable timing.

X-1 said, "Doc, we won't see you again after we land, so thanks for saving our interpreter. On behalf of all the team members, we want to thank you for coming." I shook hands with those on our chopper and told them it was an honor for me to be with the best of the best. We landed at our home base near the MASH under heavy MP guard. A commando said, "Thanks, Doc! Let's do it again sometime, okay?"

I laughed, "Thanks, but no thanks!"

CHAPTER 30

BY WAY OF THE KNIFE

We had just completed rehearsals for an overnight mission. I was to be the medic for a commando raiding party that consisted of the meanest SOBs I had ever met. All were highly skilled in their fields, outstanding night fighters, and well disciplined. As a cover for me, my company officer had been told I was needed for a while in another outfit that was short of medics.

I called it hell week. They put me through the paces—running, jumping, climbing—all in the dark, with my aid kits bouncing up and down on my backside. I had to learn each team member's medical history. Their training was one of trench warfare and hand-to-hand combat. Aerial reconnaissance photos showed a locomotive with eight railroad cars parked behind a big building about a half mile away from a small town. Intelligence had it that the railroad cars were loaded with ammo and weapons. We were to locate and destroy the train and its cargo.

The hard work was about to come into play. We were trucked from our training area in the rear echelon to an out-of-the-way field behind our front lines. We arrived at noon and met in a large tent. The whole area was guarded by military police. We wore ragged black outfits and black tennis shoes. Our faces and hands were blackened. Our leader was "Charlie." He was a full-bird colonel and a no-nonsense guy. None of the commandos had names. Charlie went over the codes for his clicker and the passwords—*silver*, counter *fox* for today and *white*, counter *eagle* for tomorrow. The code word for our mission was *Zebra*. The commandos were assigned to fifteen teams of two men each. One man was an interpreter. We had a total of thirty-three men. These guys were sharpshooters trained to penetrate enemy lines. You name the weapon or the explosives, they had it. I went over my aid kits and the special surgical kit our interpreter would carry for me.

We headed for the wire and went down to the valley below. We formed a long column, making our way through no man's land to the enemy's front line. Charlie was in the lead, the interpreter and the radioman and I were in the middle of the column. Charlie sent two of his best commandos ahead to sniff out the enemy. They could smell a rat a mile away.

We had about an hour and a half of daylight left and Charlie wanted to get through no man's land by sunset. Since we were between two large hills, we'd be in the shadows soon. We made damn good time. The tall, dense brush and the small trees were good cover. Charlie gave two clicks and the column stopped in their tracks. Charlie got on the radio to home base. "This is Zebra at 1700 hours. We made it to Point One, over and out."

Soon it was really dark. We could see only some ten feet in front of us. Charlie said, "This is it. Timing is everything. This is for all the marbles." Charlie asked me if I was ready. I said, "Let's go!"

Charlie gave one click. The men split into eight teams of four men each and moved up to the enemy's front line. As each team made it through the line, they were to give one click, the signal for the next team to go. Team 2 had the toughest part. They would go first, creeping forward on their stomachs to quietly take out whoever was in their way. They would do that by way of the knife.

We waited. Fifteen minutes went by. Then we heard one click. The next team took off. By the time the last team crossed the enemy wire, we were behind schedule. We would have to move fast to our objective. It took all I had in me to keep up with the pace. I was not a commando, I was a medic. Suddenly Charlie gave two clicks. Our point man had heard a small patrol moving in our direction. We waited. Then we heard voices. Out of the darkness came six North Korean soldiers. Charlie had given word to let them pass. The North Koreans were so close they would have stepped right on me if it weren't for the shrub between us.

We made up time reaching the outskirts of the town. Each of the teams had a designated railroad car and a specific job. First, all leaders went with Charlie to look things over while the rest of us hunkered down, hiding in the brush. The lights in the town were dim. I borrowed our radioman's high-powered night field glasses. Most of the dwellings seemed to be the small straw huts. A long dirt path led to a big one-story building with dim lights at each corner. That was where the ammo and weapons were. Four guards paced back and forth. Behind the building were the eight railroad cars and a locomotive that looked dilapidated.

Charlie's Team 1 would go first and do away with the guards. I went with them. We worked our way to the building. Charlie gave me a hand signal to stay put. With Charlie's night field glasses, I watched the guards walk from the corners of the building to meet in the middle. Team One had a split second to get into their positions at each corner. They lay flat against the building, knives drawn. When the guards reached their corners, our men silently put them away. Three clicks signaled us to move in.

The changing of guards was to be at 2400 hours—midnight. We had about three hours to pull off this job. Charlie stationed two commandos halfway down the path to cover our escape. I was to stand at a corner of the building and look like a guard. Charlie gave me an enemy helmet and a rifle. If someone from the town were to look our way, from that distance they wouldn't be able to tell I wasn't one of them. Charlie's team went to the locomotive and the first railroad car. The other teams went to their assigned cars.

Every now and then a chill ran up my spine. From where I was, I could not see the teams taping their TNT charges onto the train. I wondered how it would go, but I knew one thing—every man knew his job and could be depended upon. I hoped they all thought the same of me, but they were not very friendly, so I don't know what they thought. I also could not see the two commando lookouts halfway down the pathway. They were well concealed. From time to time I looked toward the town to see if any villagers or soldiers were roaming.

I heard a noise and pointed my rifle, but it was just Charlie and his team moving along the side of the building. I watched as the other teams joined them, placing their packs of TNT charges onto the one-story building. I waited and waited, then heard four clicks. The teams met up around me and Charlie whispered, "Doc, let's go!" I set down my helmet and rifle and scooped up my two aid kits. Off we went. We were confronted by about eight North Korean soldiers running at us, spraying bullets everywhere. With Charlie leading, we leapfrogged our way up a slight incline. From behind the incline, our teams began blasting away at the enemy.

One of the commandos had been hit in the arm. I cut open his shirt sleeve from elbow to shoulder. "Give me ten minutes," I told Charlie. After wiping up the blood with alcohol pads, I put ointment on the wound and bandaged it. "Let's go!"

One of the team leaders reported three of the North Koreans had been killed. Five had run into the building. Charlie thought they probably didn't see us setting explosives and probably just saw four of their comrades dead. Even if they found the taped explosives, it would take them a while to undo it all. The explosives were set to go off at midnight.

Now all we had to do was get out. We had a flat stretch ahead for about five hundred yards. Once through that, we'd go through a series of small hills and gullies where we could take cover from the explosion. Leading the way and at double time was Charlie. "Hang in there, Doc!"

We headed down into the first gully and got down low. I hunkered down beside Charlie. As I reached for my canteen the blast went off like a volcano eruption, so loud it seemed like the explosion was right on top of us. The sky was a rainbow of colors. Any soldiers still in the building had an immediate death. Charlie told the men, "Super job!"

Team 2 was back in the lead. I worked my way through the column to see how the commando with the arm wound was holding up. He was okay. I gave him two aspirins. We made it down a hill through thick foliage to our rendezvous area just behind the enemy front line. Charlie gave strict orders not to make any noise as we approached. If things got hot and heavy, every man knew what to do.

We heard loud voices, but could see no one. Charlie sent our interpreter and the Team 2 men to look over the area. They crawled on all fours towards the voices. Eight soldiers were ahead. Four were on line duty, the other four were nearby taking a break. They would soon relieve the men on duty.

Team 2 got the dubious honor of putting the lights out on all eight enemy. After the change of guard, it would be by way of the knife for the four closest to us, the ones going on break. With silencers on their weapons, Team 2 would then take out the four who went on line duty. With one click all teams moved forward. We stopped within twenty-five yards of their front line and Team 2 took off as the rest of us waited. We heard the three clicks, our cue to head across the line into no man's land. I crawled over two bodies.

We weren't out of trouble by a long shot. We were still in the enemy's half of no man's land. We had some two thousand yards to go before reaching our MLR. Team 2 once again took the point. We had gone halfway when one of the point men came running back saying he heard noises ahead. We hunkered down in the high grass. The sounds were getting closer. Out jumped five deer, running smack dab across our path. After that ten seconds of excitement, we took off again for home base. Once we got into our section of no man's land, Charlie got on his radio. "This is Zebra—home!" It was 0545 hours.

Charlie gave the day's password and we headed up through our minefields and through the wire. Now we had the long walk down the backside of our hill to the big tent guarded by MPs. We gathered around the tables for snacks and ice cold milk. Waiting for us was a one-star general and his aide-de-camps military assistants. We had our debriefing. We each told our stories separately, and they all needed to match up. Afterwards I went over to look at the wounded commando's arm. I put salve on it and rewrapped it. "It'll be like new in two weeks."

Charlie said, "Doc, let's do it again—okay?" I gave a thumbs up, but these commandos were hard cold killers and they hadn't really taken to me. I was an outsider to them. A helicopter came to take Charlie and his men to wherever their home base was. I would be happy to get back to my own unit.

CHAPTER 31

DEATH SURROUNDS ME

As we made our way north a bitter wind blew, ripping at our faces and ears. It was early winter. Snowflakes as big as nickels added to the already calf-high snow that covered the ground. I dreaded to think of another winter campaign. Last year, at times the wind chill and cold had gotten to minus 40 degrees or worse, and the snow might reach four to six feet within 48 hours. The forecast for this day was for snow flurries and zero degrees by nightfall. As we moved slowly around one hill and then another, we stopped periodically for brief rests and to check for any frostbite cases.

I had transferred to this outfit a week ago because they were short of medics. The platoon leader of my new company, a lieutenant, was a square dealer, a good guy. He had thanked me for coming over to help until new medics could arrive. In their last battle, this battalion had lost some 215 men. Of those who had died, five were combat medics killed by snipers while they gave aid to the wounded. Yesterday, replacement troops from a reserve battalion had arrived bringing the battalion up to near full strength for the battle coming up, but still not enough medics.

The trail leading north was a rough go with the snow and all. The battalion's objective was a hill held by the North Koreans. There was a twinge of apprehension among the new replacements. They had no idea what they were getting into, although many young soldiers thought they were immortal. Death happened to other people. The adrenalin was pumping hard and fast through these soldiers waiting for their first fight.

As we approached the hill, we heard our artillery and big mortars blasting away, softening the enemy up before our big push. We medics set up a makeshift aid station about five hundred yards from the hill. I then went back to my platoon waiting in a frozen rice paddy just west of the hill. Jump off time was set for 2130 hours. As I checked my two aid kits, a young soldier appeared out of the dark and confessed, "Doc, I'm nervous as hell." I told him things were going to be okay. I asked his squad leader if he could stick around the boy for a while, to keep him calm. The soldier was seventeen, but he looked fourteen.

Time seemed to stand still as our troops prepared to attack. For many of the new replacements, the waiting was difficult. When jump-off time arrived, our company tried to move forward up the slope of the hill, but to no avail. We were driven back by heavy mortar and machine gun fire. As the fighting raged, we knew the North Koreans were hell bent on holding their position.

The snow started falling hard again and it got colder. Mortar rounds passed overhead in both directions. The blasts of explosions mixed with the light, thin canter of enemy machine guns and the hoarse sound of our heavier caliber guns, sounding like the Fourth of July in late November. Pinned down for some twenty minutes, our troops again slowly made their way upward in the snow, going from shell hole to shell hole. To get to the top of the hill, our troops had to go through the enemy's minefield. To me, mines are among the most deadly and frightening of all weapons. It takes a special kind of courage to move through a mine area. Mines could go off even if nobody stepped on them, like if the snow got too heavy. Sure enough, one of our men got about twenty yards in when a mine went off ahead. The soldier hit the ground yelling, "Doc, come quick!"

I jumped out of the gully I was hiding in and crawled on all fours to him, using the same path through the snow that he had used. "You're damn lucky you had your flak jacket on. Lucky that mine blast was fifty yards away instead of fifty feet away." I dragged him back into the gully where I could work on him. He was full of shrapnel. I stopped all the bleeding and gave him a shot of morphine. Using tweezers, I did the best I could to pluck out the bigger pieces of shrapnel. My hands grew numb from the cold. I tagged him as WIA. The litter-bearers covered him with his poncho for the ride to our makeshift aid station.

More mines blew up around us. How many and where the mines were, no one knew, but there was no way at this point to clear them because of the deep snow. The only way to reach the wounded men was to go into the minefield. It was a matter of blind chance. I spent the next hour going in and pulling out four dead and three wounded. Of those wounded, one had his right foot blown off, one lost both legs, one lost his left arm. With the help of the litter guys, we got all three wounded bandaged, gave them morphine shots for pain, and tagged them WIA. The litter-bearers did one helluva job dodging bullets while carrying them down the hill.

The fighting stiffened and the weather worsened. I finally caught up with some of my outfit about seventy-five yards up the hill. The Lieutenant yelled, "We made it through their minefields, now let's get to the top!" That wouldn't be easy. Our troops crawled up steep, rocky slopes covered in snow. While we made slow headway, our artillery and mortar rounds smashed the enemy's snow-covered bunkers to smithereens. Our troops made it two-thirds of the way up the hill. Navigating my way through a narrow ravine with my litter-bearers, I heard "Doc, Doc!" The yell came from a shell hole about thirty yards out. I ran lickety-split through the snow towards the hole. I was met by a blast from burp gun fire above, throwing snow all around. I yelled back to my squad leader, "Help me out!"

Before I could say *jack rabbit*, a BAR man took out the shooter. When I got to our trooper, I saw he was one of our new replacements. He'd been hit in the upper left thigh. Things didn't look good for him.

I put a tourniquet on to stop the bleeding. With the help of litter guys and two BAR men covering us, we made it back to the ravine under a hail of bullets. I cut open the trooper's fatigue pants. His leg bone was splintered. With the bleeding stopped, I put sulfa powder on the wound, bandaged the soldier, and gave him morphine. "Am I going to make it, Doc?" he asked. I saw he was scared to death. "Take a deep breath. Everything will be okay. And better yet, you might be going back stateside." The litter-bearers helped me put his leg in a splint and we covered him with his poncho. I tagged him as WIA and put him in for a Purple Heart.

There was a lot more fighting to be done as well as a lot more dying. At 0300 hours the snow was still coming down and the temperature was 10 degrees below zero. As we advanced up the hill, mortars fell down on us, throwing snow high into the air. The North Koreans did not give up easily. The fighting raged for another two hours. The new snow on the hill made our upward route extremely difficult. Dodging bullets and mortars, our troops were slipping and sliding yard by yard, fighting every step of the way, taking heavy fire from above.

As we got close to the top, we found enemy bodies lying everywhere. Any wounded had frozen to death. Being a combat medic, that was the way of life—death surrounding me day in and day out. There's really no way to describe war. You've got to experience it yourself. Only those fighting on the ground know the real misery of it.

The Lieutenant ordered his troops to fix bayonets for the remaining climb to the top. The men were going to root out the enemy one by one. With frozen dripping noses and red cheeks, our platoon guys moved cautiously, crawling from one shell hole to another. The hill got steeper every step of the way. Our artillery units poured out shells ahead of us.

I had just finished tending to another wounded when our radioman yelled over. One of our squad leaders had been hit by burp gun fire and was lying out in the open. The sky was starting to lighten. Two of our troopers covered me and I made it about ten feet before a hail of bullets kicked up snow all around. Immediately our guys opened up and silenced the shooter.

The squad leader was lying still, half-covered with snow. I dragged him to a shell hole, out of the line of fire. I felt his pulse and listened for a heartbeat, but there was no indication of life. He wasn't wearing a flak jacket. I cut open his fatigue jacket, and with my penlight saw he had eight small holes in his chest made by burp gun fire, but there was little blood. He must have died instantly. Our radioman yelled over that he was one of the new replacements and some hadn't been issued flak jackets. Life is not fair. I tagged him as KIA, put one dog tag between his teeth and the other in my aid kit. I stuck the bayonet end of his rifle into the snow and set his helmet on the butt end. Then I covered him with his poncho and left him for the litter-bearers.

Daylight came. It was still snowing and below zero. At least we could now see the enemy, but they could see us as well. The Lieutenant said he didn't think the gooks could last much longer in the snow and cold with their ammo probably running short. Our battalion had umpteen amounts of everything, but you don't let your guard down for one moment. We still had a ways to go. Five hundred yards before we'd hit their trenches.

Looking up that ragged, snowy hill torn by our artillery and mortar rounds, I wondered how it would be possible to get our wounded back down and our supplies up. Our barrages hit higher and higher up the hill, our company surging upward after each, seeing more and more dead enemy frozen in the snow. Slowly our platoon moved toward the enemy trenches. The Lieutenant yelled to me, "Do you have your friend with you?"

"Yes!" The friend he was referring to was the pistol I had strapped over my shoulder. From near the crest of the hill, the North Koreans fired down at us. In a last ditch effort, our company made it up and into their trenches. Gooks jumped out and headed to the top of the hill. Bullets zipped by my head. I had just jumped into the enemy's trench to aid one of our wounded when a shattering blast hit about ten yards up. I thought I was hit, but didn't see any blood. A trooper was moaning, saying his ear drums hurt. He had been hit in the arm just below his flak jacket. The wound wasn't that bad, no broken bones and not a lot of blood lost—medics call that a clean wound. I gave him a shot of morphine for pain, although the cold weather alone might have helped with that. I cleaned the wound, dressed it, and put his arm in a sling. I tagged him as a WIA walking wounded. Off he went down to our aid station.

Our platoon could see the top of the hill some one hundred yards away. We waited on the rest of our company for the big push upward. Our artillery and mortar shells exploded onto every inch of the hilltop, snow and dirt flying. There was no resistance. When the shelling stopped, that was our cue to advance to the top. Any enemy that had survived scurried down the backside of the hill. After some seventeen hours, our battalion had the hill under control.

Looking around, I saw why there had been no resistance. Unbelievable. Hundreds of frozen bodies were stacked in the snow as far as I could see. We estimated some 1,500 dead. We medics looked into the trenches and bunkers for any enemy troops that might be wounded but alive. There were none. Our commander said we had won because we were a helluva lot better trained and better equipped—and we had better leaders than the North Koreans.

All I could think was, *Until I leave this hell on earth, death surrounds me.*

CHAPTER 32

AN ENEMY IN ITSELF

The frigid Siberian winds had been growing more brutal each day. Our battalion commander knew that soon the winter storms and big snows would come, so it was now or never that we had to take the valley. We had been fighting the North Korean forces in the mountains for the last few weeks and had pushed the remaining enemy forces down into the valley. We were as ready as we could be for the cold and snow, wearing our white snow suits and white thermal boots. I was lucky to have an old turtleneck sweater to wear, my dog tags tucked into the neck.

We stopped overnight to regroup near the valley entrance, our battalion's four companies stretched out along the mile width. Our commander and my CO agreed the North Koreans would be ready for a vigorous fight. We were in the flat lowlands now where tanks could make the difference in a heated battle. If we got through the valley, we could hunker the tanks down in the mountains on the other side and control the whole area. The tanks were Shermans with telescopic sights and 90 mm guns. They could hit a target some two thousand yards away, and small arms fire and small mortar shells had little or no effect on them. Only a big weapon of some kind could hurt them.

Before dawn, I left our company's heated headquarters tent and made my way back to my platoon. I thought about life in Korea. North Korea is a savage place. If the enemy didn't kill you, the below-zero frigid cold or the oven-like summer heat would. Everyone here hated the place. You could have dropped off the devil in the Korean summer and he would have hated it. Santa Claus and his reindeer would have hated the winter as well.

Orders were to move out at 0530 hours. Heading north, we entered what some called Death Valley. In all the back and forth fighting, many troops had tried to go through and had gotten their asses kicked. Of course, most valleys in North Korea were death valleys.

The temperature was 18 below zero. Heavy clouds and frigid winds impeded our movement and prevented any support from the air. Luckily for us, our motor pool had eight big bulldozers. They did heavy work, like clearing paths and digging holes for our troops to fight from.

Our company was met with a barrage of artillery and mortar shells. One shell landed about a hundred yards from me, throwing dirt and snow sky high and killing two of our troops. Our advance was slow and tedious. I heard a lot of noise behind me and turned, spotting two of our tanks. I felt a moment of relief. As they went by me, they traversed back and forth with their machine gun fire and gave an occasional blast from their cannons. An intrepid tank crew gave us super firepower, but the tanks were loud and the smoke from their diesel engines gave us away on any approach. The enemy would zoom in on them, which for the ground troops meant tons of artillery and mortar rounds flying in trying to knock the tanks out of commission. I had two five-men tank crews to give aid to since they were attached to our platoon.

As we pushed forward, shells exploded like we were at a fireworks show. I was passing by one of our troopers when a blast from a mortar round landed about seventy-five yards away, lifting us off the ground and throwing us down hard. After I got the cobwebs out of my head, I went to check on our man lying on a mound of dirt. He put his hand on his forehead and brought it down covered with blood, but he had only a small cut over his eyebrow—lucky him! As the trooper took off with bullets flying everywhere, I thought maybe I was living on borrowed time, too. I had suffered no injuries, just a slight concussion from the blast force.

The North Korean troops were stubbornly fighting, defending every inch of the valley, but our men were in no mood to be stopped. "Doc, over here!" A trooper pointed ahead. I found a man lying on the ground, his helmet riddled with shell fragments. I yelled for the litter-bearers. The trooper's helmet came off full of blood. He said his left leg felt numb. I looked down at the red on his white snow suit. I cut open his fatigue pant leg and found a shell fragment had pierced the back of his calf. I used a tourniquet to stop the bleeding, then cleaned and bandaged the gash on his forehead and told him I could not give him a sedative because of his head injury. As the litter-bearers took him to our makeshift aid station, a mortar shell landed twenty feet in front of one of our nearby tanks, blowing dirt, snow, and shrapnel everywhere. The tank crew was shaken, but fortunately no casualties.

Our other tank got hit topside, smoke filling the crew compartment. I jumped on top of it and pulled one of the crew up through the turret hatch and onto the ground. The other four men worked their way out seconds later, just before the tank caught fire. As we ran away, another shell hit the tank. Shrapnel went flying. The youngest man of the crew was hit bad. He wasn't wearing a helmet, just a leather tank cap. I went into action, but as fast as I worked on him I lost ground. The bleeding could not be stopped and in a few minutes he was dead.

We were now down to one tank in our platoon. To me, it takes some doing to be cooped up in a tank, with the noise and the heat inside along with poor ventilation and the stink of the diesel fuel. The tankers have to be tough, like submariners. Our tank was still burning and mortar rounds were still coming in. I ran zigzagging to a huge shell hole for cover. Jumping in, I found four of our troopers, all dead. I tagged them as KIA and took care of their dog tags.

At 1000 hours the frigid winds out of Manchuria took the thermometer down to 25 below. Frostbite cases were starting to take their toll. Keeping feet and hands dry and warm was paramount. Our frostbite cases were sent to the warming tents in the rear.

Our bulldozers went into action clearing out areas. Flatbed trucks arrived carrying mortars and artillery. By noon we were giving the North Koreans a taste of their own medicine, the roar of our mortars and artillery rounds flying over us. The barrage lasted thirty minutes or so. That gave our ground troops a chance to advance, pushing the enemy northward, further back into the valley. The skies were still too cloudy for air power.

Suddenly the North Korean troops came charging across the open valley like Custer's Last Stand. Our ground and tank machine gunners mowed them down, row after row. Each wave was beaten back. When the waves were over, the enemy dead were estimated at up to eight hundred. Our oscillating machine guns had done a good job. If the enemy got past those, our second line got 'em. Casualties by then in my platoon were five dead and twenty-two wounded.

Moving forward, we were met with sniper and automatic weapons fire. I used our tank as a shield for our wounded, even knowing that it would draw enemy fire, and it did just that. I helped pull the wounded up on top of the tank, on the flat area behind the turret, where it was easier to work on them there than on the ground in the wet snow. I worked out a plan with the tankers. If I was treating a wounded on the tank, they wouldn't fire the cannon, just their 50-caliber machine gun. Before they fired their big cannon they would open the hatch a little and wave a red flag. In that way, I knew to keep the wounded on the ground while they moved up some twenty-five yards to blast away. Anyone on top of the tank would have been thrown off. We had to stay well away from the back end of a tank when it fired because black smoke would shoot far out behind it.

I was topside of the tank treating a soldier when two infantrymen came running toward us carrying a buddy hit in both legs by burp gun fire. I yelled for our litter-bearers and finished with the soldier I was working on. We lifted the wounded man up. I had to work fast and the cold weather wasn't helping. My hands by then were pretty numb—medics couldn't always work with the special mittens on or even do much wearing gloves. I cut open the trooper's fatigue pants and put a tourniquet on each of his thighs to stop the bleeding. Thank goodness no broken bones. The litter guys cleaned up the blood while I gave the trooper a morphine shot.

"Doc, Doc!" The same two infantrymen came running back. Two of their buddies followed carrying two other wounded. Bullets flew over the tank as we gave them aid. One of these men was severely wounded. To save his buddies, he had jumped toward a grenade that had landed nearby. It exploded five feet in front of him, knocking him backward to the ground, shrapnel tearing his fatigues almost completely off. We put him up on the tank. His bulletproof vest had saved him from chest wounds, but chunks of flesh had been torn from his arms and legs. I couldn't give him morphine because he also had head wounds. The tankers threw us two blankets to wrap him in. Three of the litter-bearers helped me try to stop the bleeding and pluck out the bigger pieces of shrapnel while the other litter-bearer looked after the second man's arm wound. The shrapnel and pain were too much for the trooper. He squeezed my arm before he died. I tagged him as KIA and put him in for a Silver Star for heroism.

True to form the North Koreans stopped their attack as the valley got dark. They moved their troops closer to the safety of the hills behind them. The temperature might have had something to do with that, too. It was supposed to go down to 32 below by midnight.

We were about halfway into the three-mile-long valley. It had taken our troops twelve hours of hard fighting to get that far. We had lost about two hundred men. Many of our casualties were from frostbite—in our company alone we had lost twenty-five, my platoon of fifty-eight men had lost four. It was so damn cold that all vehicles had to be started every half hour or they would freeze up.

Sporadic weapons fire from both sides could still be heard. Our platoon leaders set up warming tents so we medics could look after our battle worn and half-frozen troops. I went around from time to time to check out our line troops and tankers as well. The frigid cold wind out of Siberia was a bitch! It blew across the valley all night at fifty to sixty miles an hour and we medics kept busy with frostbite cases. Just before dawn I heard what I thought were the sounds of burp guns from far off.

The sun came up around 0600 hours, with the temperature at thirty-two below zero as predicted. We were hoping for clear blue skies, so far so good. Yesterday's winds had vanished, leaving a cold breeze of only six miles an hour. Now we could use our air power on the enemy. Battalion knew the North Koreans had no tanks in the valley, nor any planes to back them up.

Overnight our company had lost another three to frostbite. I was in the warming tent aiding six frostbitten soldiers when our platoon runner came in with a message from the company headquarters tent. Battalion wanted to catch the enemy off guard, so an early morning air strike was called. Four waves of six planes each would drop napalm bombs. As I left the comfort of the warming tent, I looked up at the beautiful but cold clear sky. *Let's go get 'em!*

Battalion was hell-bent on getting through the valley by mid-afternoon. A twenty-five-foot-long red nylon arrow pointing north lay on the frozen ground about one hundred yards in front of our line troops so our planes wouldn't mistake us for the enemy. I asked our one and only tank group if I could use their tank again as cover for my wounded. They reminded me the tank was a target for the enemy. I strapped some medical supplies on the back of the tank and told them, "When we get out of this mess I'll give you each a beer."

"Give us a case!" they said.

"You're on!"

The planes were on their way. I hunkered down behind the tank. Out of the frozen blue skies, on the dot at 0800 hours, came the first wave of planes. They swooped down and swarmed over the valley like a bunch of locusts over a corn field. Above them was an air observation plane. Within minutes huge plumes of smoke rose throughout the valley. The planes circled the area, shooting at the enemy hiding in caves. They dropped into steep dives trying to shake off ground fire. Three more waves, then time for us to move out. It was good to hear the roar of our planes.

We had another mile and a half of fighting to get through before all the hell would be out of the way. I was sick of the slaughter and the blood and the smell, but that's war and I had a job to do. I told our squad leader that once a soldier was gone, medals and victories meant nothing to him anymore. All we could do is say thanks for serving your country. He said, "Killing is a rough and tough business. Keep your head and your ass down, Doc, we need you."

Gunfire popped in the distance as we moved further into the valley. Our planes must have done a super job because the next half mile was like a walk in the park. We saw and heard nothing of the enemy, but we still had another mile to go. Then we went over a rise and came upon hundreds upon hundreds of frozen dead bodies, many stacked ten high among piles of ammo and mortar boxes. Many of them had been burned by the napalm. It was a gruesome scene, one I'll never forget. The Lieutenant stood on the top of the tank to have a better view of the area. He shook his head, not believing what he saw.

Our advance through the rest of the valley was rapid. While I was on top of the tank aiding a soldier, our tanker buddies put the red flag out. I jumped off, dragging the wounded with me. The tank moved forward, the big cannon blasting away. The North Korean troops disappeared into the hills. They offered little resistance. The exhausted enemy soldiers had to be as cold and weary as our troops were and realized they could not win.

It was now high noon. Finally the valley was ours—a bittersweet victory. I was frozen to the bone, but my job as combat medic wasn't done yet. For the next three hours, we medics took care of 150 frostbite cases. The cold was an enemy in itself.

CHAPTER 33

AGAINST ALL ODDS

"Here on the front line, if you make just one mistake, you're dead. No second chances like on the home front, so keep your heads and butts down. Then we'll all live to see another winter day." I had just left a staff meeting in our medical aid bunker. Some of our medics were new so I reminded them that this was the big league. Everything they'd learned up to now would be put to the test.

It was zero degrees and we were on a snow-covered hill. Not a sound came from the valley below or from no man's land. For the second day in a row we saw no action in our sector of the front line. Our North Korean neighbors were on a ridge some two thousand yards away. When it was quiet at the front line, which was rare, it was for one of two reasons: the enemy was either out of ammo and waiting for more supplies, or they were getting ready for a big offensive.

Our platoon leader, the Lieutenant, had some of our new troopers come to his bunker for a pep talk. He told them, "If there's war there will be death. Don't let it be ours. Hand-to-hand combat, more than firepower, determines victory or defeat." He reminded them what Patton, the great American general, had said: "No one ever won a war by dying for their country. They won by making the other son-of-a-bitch die for his country." He ended with, "Two can play this game of killing. You can be damn sure that every gook that comes up this hill has a special pass to hell, and rest assured it's strictly a one way ticket."

Off the troopers went, back to their trench positions. I started my rounds. I liked to make my morning sick call rounds early, from 0700 hours to 0900 hours, if the battle zone permitted. When the weather got really bad, I'd see more cases of the flu. This was my day to make the rounds with our friends, the tankers attached to our unit. Our medical aid bunker was about thirty yards back on the other side of the ridge from them. The tanks were placed here and there along the ridgeline. Slots were built into the slope of the hill, just wide enough for a tank to fit. They sat in plain view of the enemy and were like sitting ducks—a very big target for the enemy mortar rounds, so they were not loved by our front line troops. The tankers were okay guys. I liked having the tanks around because we could wire to their batteries to get light to our medical aid bunker.

By 1700 hours (5:00 p.m.) it was still zero degrees. The sun had set behind our hill. It would get colder as the night went on. I was in our aid bunker checking to see if we had enough morphine since we had run out a few days back. I got a call on our sound power phone from the Lieutenant. HQ had an intelligence report. For the last four days there was some build-up of North Korean troops going on in our sector of the MLR. The Lieutenant asked if we medics had enough supplies if something came up. I said, "Everything's hunky-dory with us."

An hour later I left our aid bunker, making my way down the trench to pick up body armor a squad leader was fixing for me. On my way back, I stopped for a moment to listen. Off in the darkness of evening, I heard what sounded like the dull rumble of masses of troops coming down from the enemy's hills. The North Koreans would have to come all the way across the valley, through no man's land, and up our hill in the cold and snow of the night, although they usually preferred daytime attacks. That was a long way to come just to get killed.

Back in the aid bunker, we had finished chow and were going over medical reports when the red alert went off. Our troops ran up and down the trenches to their assigned positions. In our sector of the MLR, our trench line snaked way too far for our platoon of only fifty-seven or so to cover, but then the Brits to our left and the Turkish troops to our right had the same problem.

We medics put on our flak jackets and filled our medical bandoleers as well as our aid kits, then went to our positions on the MLR. One of our new medics looked at my pistol. He didn't have one. The new guy asked, "Have you ever had to use that?"

I said, "Only when absolutely necessary, mostly to protect the wounded. You don't have time to think, just react. It's them or me and I'm still here, but there were times when I thought I was a goner."

I was told in Army med school that fear is what keeps men alive. As a medic, my fears were running out of morphine, IVs, and blood plasma, as well as being wounded myself while giving aid. I told the new medic to always remember his job was to aid the wounded no matter what. Fear or not, nothing was going to stop me from doing my job—the troops depended on us medics.

In about an hour the North Koreans would be heading up our hill with a much bigger force than last time. From reports, about fifty thousand or so were heading toward our sector. A flare went up now and then but no enemy was in sight yet. The snow in the valley and in no man's land was about six to eight inches deep from three days ago. We knew the North Koreans would attack in continuous waves of about two thousand men each. Each wave took about thirty minutes. Twenty-five waves times thirty minutes equals a long night. This would take us to midmorning the next day if the battle lasted that long. That was their plan, to wear us down so we would surrender and go home. You could say they were the schoolyard bullies.

We had heard about some of the things our North Korean neighbors had done. They did terrible things from the beginning of the war and were still doing them. We called them "barbaric bastards," or worse. There were men, women, and little children shot in the backs of their heads, bodies put into a furnace to burn so as to hide the evidence. These were not the kind of neighbors one wants living next to them. I won't say some of what they did to our guys.

It was about 14 degrees below zero at 2130 hours (9:30 p.m.). Now we could hear little rumbles in the valley below us. White flares went up and we saw some movement of troops. We had four tanks that we didn't have last time we faced off. They would draw a lot of incoming mortars, and the North Koreans were good at firing mortars.

The first wave began firing their weapons, yelling and screaming but without all the extra gimmicks of whistles and bugles, banging drums and tin cans like the Chinese used when they attacked. We were subjected to an intense barrage. Our tanks opened up with a barrage of their own—I think it caught the enemy a little off guard. The tankers gave it all they had for ten to fifteen minutes. The noise from their blasts was deafening. They were loud, loud and loud!

One of our medics ran up to me in the trench. He had been hit while aiding a wounded. It was damn cold, but he took off his flak jacket and shirt. The bullet had hit just below his flak jacket. Lucky for him, it had just grazed him. There was a streak of blood and a small lump. I took care of the wound and told him, "You'll be okay, I'll look at it again later. Keep your ass and your head down and get back to work." Off he went. Being in a real war isn't like the movies. When guys get hit, even if it's not too bad, they want help. They discover it hurts like hell to get shot.

Shells landed up and down our trench line and beyond with a vengeance. Snow and debris flew everywhere. Body parts flew everywhere. It was a nightmare scene. At times our hill was an inferno of exploding shells. The enemy that made it up through our minefields reeked of garlic. When they got closer to our MLR they were like quail running in all directions getting picked off by our troops.

I finally made it up to a wounded man calling for help. "Doc," he cried, "I can't stand the pain!" A grenade had ripped him open and exposed his intestines. I yelled for the litter-bearers and then gave him a shot of morphine. I pressed his intestines back into his body. When the litter-bearers arrived, we put two extra-large battle dressings around the soldier. "Hang in there, this is all I can do for now." He squeezed my hand and then went limp. I tagged him KIA and the litter-bearers covered him with his poncho and took him away.

Mortars started coming in salvo after salvo. I had to get the hell out of there fast. I ran down the trench. A huge blast landed in the area I had just been in and knocked me flat. I lay face down in the trench for what seemed like forever. I had sunk into the snow and that probably helped protect me.

The battle raged on through the night and into the early morning. The enemy fired everything they had, kitchen sink and all. I heard more and more calls for "Doc!" and was covered with blood from head to toe. Then the fighting intensified. Some of the enemy penetrated our trench line. Our men fought hand-to-hand, hunting them down and killing them by knife or bayonet. Most, though, never made it through our minefield or the barbed-wire along our MLR. Our machine gunners, all eight of them, were having a field day. Hordes of snow-covered bodies lay everywhere. I ducked into our medical aid bunker to restock with morphine, battle-dressings, and other supplies. I took off my mittens so I could wipe off blood that had soaked through to my hands, which were numb from the 20 below zero weather. With my two aid kits refilled, I put on a new pair of mittens and took off for the next call for help.

The Land of the Morning Calm was not at all calm. Bullets ricocheted everywhere. The North Koreans were still on the move, continuously working their way up the snow-covered valley in waves that looked to be endless. Many of their wounded had frozen to death from the bitter cold. Dawn was only an hour away. I wondered how much longer the enemy was willing to be slaughtered like animals. This wasn't war, this was madness. There had been some fourteen waves and thousands dead or wounded. Still they came for more punishment.

I had just finished patching up a soldier when I heard a bugle blowing from far off. The waves of troops, including the one working their way up our hill, stopped and headed back. It was all over at 0530 hours, some eight hours after the battle had started. Our tanks took one last blast at the enemy as they retreated.

There was a virtual carpet of North Korean dead. One could walk the entire seventy-five yards in front of our MLR on bodies and not leave a footprint in the snow. We survived and they didn't because our troops were better trained and better equipped. Our troops wore body armor and theirs did not. Most of their troops didn't even wear helmets. Of the fifty-seven men we had in our platoon, nine were dead and sixteen wounded, leaving thirty-two battle-weary, hungry, frostbitten troopers. I don't know how many casualties there were in the other platoons. One of the dead was my good buddy. He was nineteen years old and one helluva medic. In spite of our heavy loss, we managed to hold onto our section of the MLR against all odds.

CHAPTER 34

CODE RED

For the past three days we had been trading blows—the Chinese wanted our mountain. We were up on one of the highest hills on our way north, fighting in some of the worst winter elements. Ten inches of snow had fallen the night before, and eight more inches of the powdery stuff last night. The snowflakes were as big as quarters, at times as big as half dollars. Now we had lingering flurries plus bitter winds blasting about 55 miles per hour out of the north.

I was about halfway through my morning medical rounds when our company runner came into the snow-packed trench yelling that our CO, the Captain, wanted to see me. By the time I got to the CP bunker, all the leaders from the battalion were there. My platoon leader, the LT, said, "Doc, things don't look good."

The Captain put a large map on the table and got right to the point. "This is big… very big. A massive enemy build-up has been in the making for the last week and a half. Chinese troops are assembling behind the hill next to us with a force of some 500,000 men." He warned us that our sector of the front line most likely would take the brunt of attack. From now on, our outfit was under Code Red, and we were to be alert and ready for action. The Captain told me, "I hope the medics will all wear their sidearms. They may need them."

By the time I left the bunker, the temperature had dropped five more degrees, with more snow flurries. I went over medical plans with all medics and litter-bearers. I reminded everyone that our battalion surgeon had said frostbite accounted for more American casualties in our first winter of combat than the enemy. From my own experience, I knew a needle wouldn't go into a soldier's arm or leg if the skin was too frozen—it'd break right off. I told our medics that if that happened, they were to get the wounded down the back slope of our hill to the heated medical bunker as fast as possible. I told them to strap on a sidearm because the Chinese played by no rules.

I headed to the front line to see how the troops were holding up in the bitter cold and snow. Stockpiles of ammo were covered with waterproof tarp. Our company had sixteen tanks attached, four for each platoon, and they had stockpiled their own ammo. I checked on the tankers, too. A buddy medic and I were covering all four areas of our sector, some three hundred yards of zigzagging trenches. We were short three medics from our last engagement fourteen days ago.

When I returned to my bunk, the LT called in to say Intelligence had sighted Chinese forces heading toward all sectors of our battalion's MLR. Estimated arrival was in about four hours—just in time for a night battle, their favorite time to attack. I put on my shoulder holster with my .45.

One of our platoon squad leaders rang in to say a man was down sick in Area 3. The trooper was in a lot of pain. His temperature read 103.7 degrees. Feeling his abdomen, I diagnosed an inflammation of his appendix and told the squad leader to radio in to our battalion surgeon to get ready for an appendectomy. Litter-bearers took the man down our back slope to a waiting jeep.

Darkness was coming, and I expected the Chinese to show up like clockwork with their band of instruments announcing *ready or not, here I come*. I peeked out of the medical bunker a few times but things were pretty quiet, just the light snow falling. The silence was eerie as we waited. The temperature had dropped to 37 below zero—damn cold in any language.

Then in the distance we heard it. Bugles blowing, the shrill sound of whistles, the banging of drums, sound blasting from all directions. The blackness of the night concealed the enemy advance. The LT looked at his watch . . . yes, like clockwork. All four platoons sent up white flares and the sky lit up like it was day. Before us was a mass of Chinese making their way across the valley to our hill in a scene you had to see to believe. Our 1,075 men were vastly outnumbered. As the flares went out one by one, our front line fired into the darkness.

One of our trip-flares went off, which meant the first wave was at the bottom of our hill. That was the signal for the enemy's big guns. Shells landed everywhere, many of them coming short of their target—us—and landing on their own men. Up through our minefields came the first wave. Farmers, old men, women, and children stepped on our mines and were hit by their own shells and artillery. Behind them came the soldiers. As fast as our gunners loaded, they fired, spraying the waves with .30 and .50 caliber rounds. Civilians and enemy dropped like flies. We were taking a lot of casualties. I had more wounded on my hands than I could handle. The enemy marched methodically and our troops stubbornly held their ground. Our big artillery rounds came so fast they lit up the valley. What an awesome, terrible barrage.

I made my way through a snow-covered trench, bullets flying overhead, shells landing all around. I had just patched up a wounded in Area 3 and heard a call from Area 1. One of our riflemen had a severely sprained ankle. The same ankle he had sprained a few times before. Our litter guys took him down the back slopes. An artillery round exploded ahead of me. I found the mangled bodies of our two machine gunners. I yelled for our platoon squad leader who came and took over one of the machine guns.

Our troops moved up and down the trenches, trying to give the Chinese the impression we were fully manned. The booming of unrelenting gunfire and explosions rolled across the valley while flares burst high in the air. I finished working on a wounded hit in both legs, and as the litter-bearers carried him away the tank commander yelled, "Doc, stay clear! It's showtime!"

On command, all four tanks blasted their 90mm cannons in a thundering barrage. Bodies flew everywhere, but as hundreds fell, hundreds more moved upward. After a long fifteen minutes, the tanks stopped firing and their turret hatches popped open. The tank commander stuck his head out of one and yelled for me. Once the black smoke cleared, I jumped onto the snowy top of the tank. "Doc," he said, "I need a couple aspirins."

As I reached into my aid kit, a bullet zinged off the turret. The tank commander pulled out his .45 and silenced the shooter. I handed him the aspirins and jumped off the tank, heading for the MLR. As I got there, the entire line erupted with rifle fire and bursts from machine guns. Our big mortars and artillery rounds produced gaping holes in the enemy's formation.

By midnight the temperature hit 45 below zero. The barrels of two of our machine guns overheated and warped. Two reserves were brought in to continue spraying the slopes with deadly fire. Still heavily outnumbered, our troops fought with all they had. Still the Chinese came wave after wave. They meant to overwhelm us with manpower, the attacks stretching our line troops dangerously thin at times. Pitiful cries for help came from everywhere. To get from one end of the trench to the other, I had to crawl over our own dead and dozens of dead Chinese that had run through our MLR. The smell of fresh blood was sickeningly strong.

I worked my way down the trench to Area 4. Overhead, shrapnel sang its deadly melody. One of our riflemen thought his buddy was dead. He was. He had a single bullet to the head and had probably died instantly. I covered him with his poncho and stuck the bayonet of his rifle into the snow, his helmet over the butt end. I was tending a badly wounded with a big piece of shrapnel in his leg when a concussion grenade exploded nearby. I came to and saw my wounded lying in the snow half dazed. The litter-bearers arrived and we all hunkered low, bullets ripping over our heads and mortars throwing dirt. I finished bandaging the wounded. I couldn't give him a shot of morphine because his arms and legs were frozen. I couldn't give him an aspirin because my canteen water was frozen and in his state he might choke on swallowing a pill dry. But, if it hadn't been for the sub-zero weather, he might have bled to death.

For the next hour and a half our troops met and exceeded their test of courage. The sound of automatic weapons fire was deafening. Our tanks went into action again, blasting away at onrushing Chinese. One Chinese jumped into the trench with me and I flew like a bat out of hell, zigzagging while bullets kicked up snow behind me. I was damn glad for his bad aim and for my bulletproof vest. The Chinese was about thirty feet behind me when I turned a corner. I hit the ground and waited, my .45 ready. As he came into sight, I pulled the trigger and he fell face down. I waited a bit, and when he didn't move I slowly got up, my .45 pointed in case he was playing dead, as sometimes they did. I rolled him over with my foot. "Great shot, Doc!" Our squad leader stood above me. He had watched it all from above the trench. I put my weapon back into its holster and went on to another cry for help.

We were going on 0330 hours and the temperature had hit 57 below zero. I was tending to two troopers with frostbite. The litter-bearers showed up and hustled both men back to the heated rear aid bunker. I heard again the sound of bugles and whistles. Flares shot up, our line troops got a clear look and opened fire at another wall of attacking Chinese. As the morning went on, the Chinese who had survived our onslaught began to withdraw, evacuating what they could of their casualties.

At dawn the sun barely peeked through the clouds, then spurts of snow flurries fell again. A half hour later, the sun shone through, displaying the horrible bloodbath. The mutilated and frozen bodies of thousands of Chinese littered the hillside in front of us. Arms and legs were frozen in midair, a sight I'll never forget. After twelve hours of nonstop fighting, all was over. It was a wonder any of us had made it. I felt someone must have been watching over me.

CHAPTER 35

UNBELIEVABLE CARNAGE

Our whole sector was on red alert. Intelligence reports had come down from Division saying tonight the Chinese were planning an attack along our front line with a force of 50,000 to 100,000 troops. All companies were planning for all contingencies. Our platoon leader, the LT, had his troops pile ammo knee-deep up and down our trenches. To get to us, the Chinese had to climb our big, steep hill full of minefields and booby-traps. Orders were for all troops to fix bayonets for the coming confrontation. But first things first for me.

On this day in late January, the temperature was 5 degrees and expected to drop to below zero by noon. I had just strapped on my aid kits and was ready for morning sick-call rounds when the LT called me on our sound power phone. He wanted to tag along to give support to the men. I met him in the trenches at Position 1 and he spoke to the troopers as I went around checking on them. After a while he said, "Doc, I notice a lot of the men have condoms stretched over their rifle muzzles to keep them dry. Where in the hell did they get them?"

I said, "From us medics. We pass them out when they go to Japan on R&R and they keep the extras and use them on their rifles. They take them off before firing their weapons." The LT laughed and then took off. I finished my rounds without him and went back to our aid bunker to load up my aid kits for the night's engagement.

We had a staff meeting for all medics and litter-bearers. I said, "The gravest threat in our serious wound cases is shock. Let's give priority to abdominal wounds and bone fractures." I went off to check on a platoon that was short of medics, then headed back down the trench to my platoon. I ran into one of our squad leaders shooting the bull with a couple machine gunners. I told them, "I got one of those new types of bulletproof vests three weeks ago. Hope I don't have to put it to the test tonight." The Army used several styles of body protection, from older heavy Doron-plated vests to newer designs of lighter weight nylon types.

The rest of the day went by uneventfully. By 1915 hours (7:15 p.m.) the snow had stopped. Minutes ticked by with agonizing slowness. At 1945 hours we heard the sound of troops marching in the snow in the valley below. Round after round of incoming mail landed all the way onto the back slopes of our hill. After about five minutes, all went silent. We knew what was coming next—it was like a Hollywood script. A rush of farmers and town folks charged us, screaming and yelling their way through our minefields, waving broomsticks to look like rifles. Mixed in with them were Chinese troops chasing them and firing weapons. Then the mass of Chinese troops came, yelling and screaming. They covered the whole snow-white valley below. They wore tennis shoes, most without socks. Many had no gloves. Some had hats or caps but no helmets. Thousands came streaming up our hill. Our firing and shelling lit up the night.

Our squad leaders ran up and down our trench line yelling for the men to fix bayonets and hold their fire until the enemy got to within one hundred yards of our line. Enemy mortars came flying in, more landing all the way on our back slopes. We hunkered down in the trenches. Our machine gunners zeroed in on any enemy making it through our minefields, cutting them down by the hundreds as they rushed our MLR. The terror-filled shrieks of bayoneted enemy could be heard up and down our trenches.

As I gave aid to one of our wounded, the trooper whispered, "Doc, we got company!" By the time I looked up it was all over. One of our riflemen had jumped into our trench and thrust his bayonet through the chest of a Chinese running at me. The enemy fell dead just feet away. I heard Sarge yelling to his troops, "The ones that get through our minefield, let 'em get within fifty meters before blasting away. Use your machine guns, and start throwing hand grenades."

There were dead Chinese, or parts of Chinese, all over our hill and in the trenches. Bodies lay as far down the forward slope as we could see. The carnage was unbelievable. Our own wounded were scooted off down our back slopes. The waiting litter jeeps hauled them to the battalion aid station. By now I had aided some thirty-five wounded. From time to time, we heard cries for help coming from below. Our interpreter said the Chinese were yelling for medical help. But they had no medics. They were left to die.

Bullets whizzed overhead. "Here they come again!" Our troops waited in the trenches with fixed bayonets. I and another medic hunched down near one of our bunkers, staying as low as we could. Hand-to-hand combat broke out, Chinese everywhere. The trench fight lasted some twenty minutes. Bodies lay in and over the trenches. A voice called, "Help, Doc, help, Doc!"

A buddy medic and I made our way toward the cry, trying not to step on bodies, but they were impossible to avoid. As we got near the voice we ran into another pile of bodies. The voice yelled, "Here, Doc!" We found two of our troopers lying under five dead, bayoneted Chinese. We pulled them out. One of the troopers had died from a bayonet wound to the abdomen. The live one yelling to us had a bayonet wound through his upper thigh. I cut open his bloody fatigue and told him I was sorry about the cold. My buddy medic put on a tourniquet to stop the bleeding, then gave a shot of morphine. The gash was long and deep. I yelled for four litter-bearers. While the other medic held the tourniquet tight, I put four battle dressings on the wound. As my buddy medic tagged him as WIA, I told him to write the soldier in for a Silver Star as well as a Purple Heart. I told the litter-bearers, "Watch the tightness of the tourniquet. He's going to need whole blood right away."

It was damn cold, 21 below zero now at 0345 hours. Our hands and feet were numb, but we couldn't stop to warm up. There were too many wounded to tend to. I told my buddy medic to set up a makeshift aid station in a bunker closer to the MLR and to get two riflemen to guard it. He could work out of there while I tended to the wounded in the trenches.

The fighting had gone on for about eight hours with no let-up. The other platoons in our company were having problems as well. I thought I heard another cry for help so I worked my way up the trench, shells blasting overhead throwing snow sky high. I came across one soldier slumped over, covered with blood from head to toe. He wasn't the only soldier lying in the trench. There were six others—all dead Chinese. I looked up and saw more dead Chinese. Six more lay on the snow-covered ground in front of me. I yelled for the litter-bearers and they came running.

The trooper had multiple gunshot and stab wounds. I cut open his uniform and found his intestines outside his belly. "Hang in there," I said, but I knew he was dying. He was in heavy shock and probably couldn't hear me. All I could do was make him comfortable in his last minutes, so I gave him a shot of morphine and wrapped him in his poncho. I put his head in my lap. He clutched my hand and died. I tagged him KIA. Heading back down through the trench, I heard one helluva lot of gunfire from Position 3, about fifty yards down. Our squad leader yelled, "Stay low!"

Sarge and two of his men were chasing six Chinese down the trench. The enemy slipped into one of our bunkers. Sarge jumped on top of the bunker, pulled the pin on a grenade, dropped it into an opening, and shut the trap door. Boom! The explosion ripped the door off, smoke boiling up. As the smoke cleared, Sarge and his men jumped into the bunker. The inside was in shambles, rubble everywhere. The Chinese lay in a heap in the corner.

The first hint of daybreak was about thirty minutes away, but flares lit the sky like it was already morning. A giant explosion rocked the valley below us. Our artillery guns pouring down a rain of fire and steel on the closely packed Chinese must have hit a pile of their ammo. I was about to tag a couple of our wounded when someone yelled, "Take cover!" About a dozen Chinese with burp guns had overrun our trench lines. I lay as flat as I could in the shadows of the trench and waited. In about twenty minutes, it was all over. I yelled for four litter-bearers to meet me in Position 6 nearby. When I got there it was one helluva scene. Bodies littered the trench. There was just enough morning light by then to make out who was who. Lying in the bloody snow were twelve dead bayoneted Chinese, along with two of our own dead bayoneted men. I had the litter guys go check our wounded, to see in what order I should tend to them.

Combat medics are trained to do whatever has to be done whenever it needs to be done, regardless of the situation. This was one of those times. As gruesome as it was, I pulled the bayonets out of our two dead men. Then I cut their dog tags off, one going in my aid kit, the other between their teeth. The litter-bearers went back and forth carrying six wounded and the two dead down the backside of our hill. They covered the dead with their ponchos.

Shells flew over us sending shrapnel zipping over our heads. Wham! Bang! Boom! Crash! The Chinese hit us with every mortar shell they had. For almost forty-five minutes a barrage of all calibers came at us. The LT came over to talk to our squad leader. He said it was unusual for the Chinese to fight past dawn. This hill we took from them a few weeks ago had to be very important for them to fight like this, but why? Mortars were still coming in. There was no end to the stream of Chinese coming up our hill. The fighting during the early morning was bitter, often man-to-man in our sector. The cold was vicious, the ground snowy. Our defense was tenacious and we had taken a significant bite out of their attack. Surely the Chinese could see the horror, the wastefulness of their fight. Our noses dripped and our cheeks were red. Our hands and feet were numb. Our machine gunners were pissed off by the damn cold, and to make things worse it began to snow again, obscuring their vision. The Chinese kept up an almost continuous barrage of mortars. They wanted that hill, and bad. But we, too, wanted the hill. It would put us closer to their capital, Pyongyang.

Snow was falling at about an inch an hour. The LT thought the Chinese had slowed their upward movement toward us. Maybe, just maybe, the shelling was their last hurrah. Then we heard tooting horns and blowing bugles—the retreat of remaining thousands. They headed back down into the valley and across no man's land to the hills beyond. The frigid weather along with the falling snow might have played a big part in their decision to call it a day, so to speak. It was 0900 hours.

I could still hear calls of "Doc, Doc, up here!" As I headed toward the cries I asked a couple litter-bearers to stop at our aid bunker and pick up an extra satchel or a bandolier of equipment I could sling over my shoulder. My aid kits were running damn low.

It took all of an hour and a half for the retreating enemy to clear out of the valley with the help of our artillery and mortar rounds. They had thousands of losses. All was not good for our home team either. Our total losses amounted to eighty or more dead and some one-hundred and fifty wounded. As the litter guys carried the most badly wounded down the back slopes, we medics helped the walking wounded to the bottom of the hill. All the wounded were then put in waiting litter jeeps. We medics headed down the snowy road to our battalion aid station a half mile away to re-stock our aid kids and grab more medical supplies and equipment for our aid bunker. We had to get ready for our next engagement. As we climbed back up our hill, loaded with supplies, I yelled to my buddy medics, "War is hell!"

Korean War Memorial, Washington D.C.
Library of Congress, Prints and Photographs Division

CHAPTER 36

LAST WORDS

The Korean War ended in an armistice signed on July 27, 1953. No formal peace treaty. The 38th parallel is a demilitarized zone between communist North Korea and democratic South Korea. When I got back home from the Korean War in the spring of 1953, I took some much needed time off for "rest and recuperation." My fingers were blackened from frostbite and I could hardly move them. My feet and ankles were affected, too. The VA docs didn't really know what to do for that, so I soaked my hands and feet in warm water two or three times a day. In about a year and a half, my circulation came back well enough that I started rewriting my notes by hand. Some were faded from rain or snow. I rewrote them the best I could.

Returning to civilian life was hard. To go from constant violent trauma to quiet living is a shock. Combat changes people—some then, some later. When I am alone, my mind sometimes wanders back to Korea. To this day I am still a little jittery and jumpy. I don't sleep a lot. I have problems with tinnitus, ringing in my ears. In quiet times, I can hear the persistent peppering of artillery and mortar rounds and sharp gunfire. I remember the injured and wounded, the blood and body parts. Until some years ago, I had troubles with flashbacks, when it seemed I was actually living those times again. I didn't want to talk about it. I didn't think anyone would understand anyway. I hoped they would not understand—I wouldn't wish that on anyone.

You don't forget the sounds completely. You can't forget war. Nightmares haunt me to this day. They are always the same ones. I call them my seven demons. I've learned to control them to a point. That's a work in progress. Sometimes even now when I watch TV, like a tennis match, suddenly the screen becomes a battlefield. When I started rewriting my notes, I often had to take a few days off because remembering was too much. Why did I survive? Out of all the horrors of war, the guilt of survival is what haunts me most. I will never know why I lived when so many others did not.

Some of the men told me they got together and put me in to get a Bronze and a Silver Medal, even a Medal of Honor as well as a Purple Heart for a shrapnel wound in my foot, but I never got any of them. The officer on duty when I signed off on my papers to leave Korea was a tough old major. The guys in line ahead of me warned me as they came out of his office. "You'll see." He thought medics didn't need any medals. He said any medic who couldn't take care of himself didn't deserve a Purple Heart. I didn't want any medals anyway. I did my job. My war records were burned up in the big 1973 fire at the St. Louis Personnel Records Center. All I have left are my notes and my dog tags and a few bad copies of photos, and in 2010, the sixtieth anniversary of the start of the war, I got a letter from the president of South Korea thanking me for my service.

War means kill or be killed. You don't forget when you see men killed in front of you day in and day out, especially when it's your friends. In my black book, which I kept in my aid kit, I wrote the names, addresses, and phone numbers of those who had asked me to contact their families if something happened to them. I had promised them I'd call, write, or visit each of their families. And I did. I told each family what their son had asked me to tell them. That included the truth of how they had died and their last words. Many men died in my arms. Some died on the stretchers as we readied them for transport to the battalion aid station or MASH. Below are some of those last words. I didn't include names. They were all heroes. Heroes never give up. Don't you ever give up.

God bless America
Tell my family, I love them all
See you in Heaven
Give 'em hell, Doc
Tell my wife I love her
Tell my mom she's the best
Why me—I'm only seventeen
Tell my sis to hang in there
Did we kick their butts?
Give my dog tags to my family
I hope I didn't let the troops down
What a bitch of a way to die
Hold me, Doc
Did we take the hill?
Tell my family how I died
Thanks for everything, Doc
Give me the last rites, Doc
Tell my family I'll watch over them
I don't want to die in this God-forsaken place
I don't want to die alone
Tell LT I took out the tank
Tell my fiancée I'm sorry
Tell the guys I love them all
Tell my Dad I'm not coming home
Tell everyone war is hell

I didn't come home with a chest full of medals for bravery, but I did come home with a chest full of pride for what I had done in saving lives.

BATTLEFIELD PRAYER

Soldiers dying on the battlefield would sometimes ask me to pray for them. This was what I said:

You gave all you had while here on earth.
You are now going to a place where there is no such thing as time,
only Everlasting Peace.
Amen

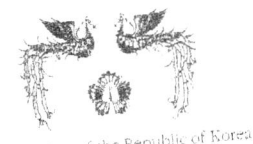

The President of the Republic of Korea

June 1, 2010

William J. 'Andy' Anderson

Dear William J. 'Andy' Anderson,

This year as we commemorate the sixtieth anniversary of the outbreak of the Korean War, we honor your selfless sacrifice in fighting tyranny and aggression. We salute your courage in enduring the unimaginable horrors of war. We pay tribute to your commitment in protecting liberty and freedom.

We Koreans made a promise to build a strong and prosperous country that upholds peace and freedom so that the sacrifices that you made would not have been in vain. We have faithfully kept that promise. Korea today is a vibrant democracy with a robust economy and we are actively promoting peace and stability around the world. Korea transformed itself from a country of received aid to one that provides aid to others. We are proud of what we managed to accomplish and we wish to dedicate these achievements to you.

The Korean government has been inviting Korean War veterans every year as part of its Revisit Korea Program since 1975. This year we will be inviting 2,400 Korean War veterans and their families. We Koreans and myself in particular look forward to welcoming you. We hope that you will see what you made possible and hope that your families will feel renewed pride in what you did for us many years ago.

Please accept, once again, our warmest gratitude and deepest respect. You will always remain our true Heroes and we assure you that we will continue to do our best to make you proud. On behalf of the Korean people, I would like to say "Thank you."

Sincerely yours,

Lee Myung-bak
President, Republic of Korea

GLOSSARY

artillery – large military weapons that can fire long range

BAR – Browning Automatic Rifle

BAS – battalion aid station

battalion – military unit of three to four companies, usually led by a lieutenant colonel

Bronze Star – military award for heroism in combat

bulletproof vest – sturdy form of body armor protecting against bullets

bunker – above ground fortified or underground structure to protect soldiers

burp gun – submachine gun used by Chinese and North Korean forces

C-ration – pre-cooked, packaged meal for military field use

CCF – Chinese Communist Forces

CO – commanding officer

CP – command post

casualties – refers to both wounded and killed

Chink – slang name for a Chinese soldier

church key – can opener

commandos – special operations soldier

commo wire – heavy wire used in communication lines

company – military unit of three to four platoons, usually led by a captain or major

corpsman – enlisted medical specialist trained in Navy schools

Corsair – type of propeller-driven American fighter plane

craps – game of tossing dice and gambling on outcome, "shooting craps"

fix bayonets – to attach the bayonet knife to the end of the rifle

flak jacket – form of body armor protecting against shrapnel

flamethrower – backpack device that shoots a long stream of fire through a tube

front line – the military's forward position

full bird – a colonel, insignia is an eagle

G2 – military intelligence

gold leaf – a major, insignia is a gold leaf

gook – slang name for a North Korean soldier

HQ – Army Headquarters

howitzer – long-barreled artillery weapon, usually mounted on wheels

Intelligence – military branch collecting information on the enemy

KIA – killed in action

LT – lieutenant

leapfrogging – to jump forward in a zigzag pattern as a tactic to avoid being shot

MLR – main line of resistance, also called the front line or the wire

MP – military police

medevac – medical evacuation by helicopter

medic – enlisted medical specialist trained at various Army schools

mop up – after a battle, looking for any wounded enemy left behind

mortar – artillery weapon that shoots mortar bombs through a tube

napalm – highly flammable, very hot-burning gel-like substance

no man's land – area between the front lines of opposing sides

penlight – small, pen-sized flashlight

perimeter – guarded boundary line around an area of troops

platoon – military unit of at least two squads, usually led by a lieutenant

point man – a scout or leading soldier (also "take the point")

police up – clean up the area of debris

Purple Heart – military award for those wounded or killed in combat

ROK – Republic of Korea army (South Korean)

recon – reconnaissance, the gathering of information about an enemy's presence

scuttlebutt – rumor

shoot the bull – chatting

shrapnel – flying projectiles resulting from explosions of bombs, shells, or mines

silver leaf – a lieutenant colonel, insignia is a silver leaf

Silver Star – military award for gallantry in combat (higher award than the Bronze Star)

skivvies – underwear

small arms – small weapons such as pistols, rifles, light machine guns

sound power phone – field telephone run by a battery and connected to other phones by heavy communication wire (commo wire) squad – smallest military unit, usually led by a sergeant

trench – long ditch dug to protect soldiers

trip wire – wire attached to an explosive device

WIA – wounded in action

weapons carriers – smaller, open bed army trunks that transport weapons and their crews

web belt – webbed-cotton belt on which looped pouches, cases, or holsters can be strung

wire – rolls of barbed wire strung along the front line position

www.ingramcontent.com/pod-product-compliance
Lightning Source LLC
Chambersburg PA
CBHW050631300426
44112CB00012B/1747